MEYER DAVIS
MADE TO MEASURE

MEYER DAVIS
MADE TO MEASURE
ARCHITECTURE AND INTERIORS

WILL MEYER and GRAY DAVIS

TEXT BY
DAN SHAW

FOREWORD BY
DAVID NETTO

THE VENDOME PRESS
NEW YORK

CONTENTS

FOREWORD

It's not enough to just be "modern" today—there's plenty of that. Now that nearly seventy years have passed since Mies van der Rohe's Farnsworth House and almost fifty since Charles Gwathmey's house for his parents—and with McMansion versions of both iconic buildings littering the fields of Long Island—really good architecture and design in a contemporary style has to have a *voice*. Something a bit richer than the orthodox sleekness of glass curtain walls and Mies chairs.

Will Meyer and Gray Davis of Meyer Davis are certainly contemporary designers, but they work in a vocabulary that changes from project to project and seems to have no particular aesthetic as a design goal. One of the reasons for this open-mindedness in their work may be that despite their training as architects, they are not preoccupied with form. They are as interested in interior design as in the architectural envelope, and value atmosphere and sensuality (the role of lighting, say, or texture) over the physical identity of a building. They are designers of *environments*, and the point of their work, which can be delivered in many forms, is the pursuit of happiness in the user. Perhaps they learned this early in their careers, when Will worked for Charles Gwathmey and Gray for the distinguished decorator John Saladino.

Meyer Davis has accumulated a very successful body of retail, hotel, and residential work in the last fifteen years, but to one question it is hard to picture the answer: Do clients know what they want when they call them? Or what they will get?

The result, as Oscar de la Renta found, may come in the exotic form of coquina walls (a finish for the Oscar boutiques that Meyer Davis has trademarked all over the world); the drama of floor-to-ceiling tile for restaurants like Bowery Meat Company and St. Cecelia; or (as I myself discovered in one of several collaborations with Meyer Davis) the intimacy and simplicity of bleached fir boards to clad the interior of a beach house.

Of all our collaborations, some with really wonderful clients and some less so, the renovation of my house in Amagansett has been the most meaningful for me. This is because it is a very difficult and personal thing to do a house for oneself, and if you are not a designer consumed with ego, it can be fun to look at your own life through the eyes of a friend. It was Will and Gray who suggested we do the project, as a bet (they bet me we could make my house beautiful without tearing it down, and I disagreed). Also, I firmly believe that every designer should, for practice, walk a mile in the clients' shoes and have the experience of paying the astonishing bills that go along with any comprehensive renovation; the *costs* of making these dreams we love to sketch become real. It makes you a better

manager of other people's projects—and insisting on value makes you a better designer too. I have called this house many times a happiness *machine*, and the results Meyer Davis achieved were well worth the money. I can also say that working together has only strengthened my friendship with Will and Gray.

The experience of working on my house was a good one for them as well, because soon after the project was finished, Will bought a house in the neighborhood and redid it spectacularly, drawing upon the existing design by Hugh Newell Jacobson and adding to it in a very sophisticated way. So far I have been unsuccessful in persuading Gray to move to the South Fork of Long Island, but when you see in these pages the house he shares with his partner, Chase Booth, in Copake, New York, you will understand why.

As this book confirms, with finishes or forms Meyer Davis is not afraid to take a chance. Will and Gray like to play with opposites and conjure beauty by contrast, putting wood in a skyscraper and maybe a little strong marble in a log cabin. The results are consistently chic, charismatic, and—perhaps most consistently—humane. They are *humane* modernists. Being from the South helps anyone get an early start on an instinct for hospitality, but their natural warmth is innate, regionless, and could as easily have originated in Scandinavia or any other part of the world known for its facility in the making of happy environments (the architectural critic Paul Goldberger once wrote that a walk in the company of Rafael Moneo up and down the lobby of Harvard's Graduate School of Design turned the space on a dreary Cambridge day into "the sunniest piazza in Spain"—one of my favorite lines about architecture anywhere). Coming from a fellow designer who is still happy to have lost that bet, most complimentary of all might be to say that Will and Gray's style is original but, in the end, also seems inevitable, and after you see a project by Meyer Davis you think, "Why didn't I think of that?"

David Netto
2016

PAGE 12

David Netto's living room, Amagansett, New York.

OPPOSITE, CLOCKWISE FROM TOP LEFT

Gray Davis's Greenwich Village apartment, New York City; Will Meyer's dining room, Williamsburg, Brooklyn; Gray Davis's Island House on Copake Lake in upstate New York; Will Meyer's beach house in East Hampton, New York.

INTRODUCTION

Whenever you're in a hotel, restaurant, or boutique designed by Meyer Davis, you feel as if you're on a zip line traversing the zeitgeist. Will Meyer and Gray Davis create private and public interiors that stimulate neurons, arouse the senses, and make the heart do somersaults. Since establishing their New York City firm at the dawn of the millennium, they've become pivotal players in the hospitality and retail worlds, elevating standards and expectations by creating seductive, uber-stylish places to dine, shop, and sleep.

Will and Gray's vast portfolio of residential projects in both city and country informs their commercial work—and vice versa. Hotel suites are as soothing and luxurious as private clients' bedrooms. Restaurants have curated collections of paintings, photographs, and decorative objects that express their personality and individuality. Lobbies and cocktail lounges are as well appointed and conducive to conversation as the most congenial living rooms.

Will and Gray are able to work all over the world because they are fluent in a range of architectural vernaculars. They are storytellers who create a narrative for each project that dictates the design process from beginning to end. Every commission is site specific and made to measure. Their versatility is evident, for example, at the W Chicago Lakeshore and the 1 Hotel South Beach; both are enormous waterfront hotels, but they couldn't be more dissimilar. A contemporary "farmhouse" with glass walls in Tennessee is a radical yet logical response to a totally private location with open views in every direction, while a new townhouse on Manhattan's Upper East Side blends in with its nineteenth-century neighbors, though it's strikingly twenty-first century on the inside. Every project is a dissertation on the sociology of place.

The psychology of hospitality is key to their approach and success. Graciousness is not a concept but a way of life they learned by osmosis as children growing up in genteel precincts of the American South. Both natives of Tennessee, they met at the Auburn University College of Architecture, Design and Construction, where they received bachelor's degrees in architecture. But it was not until they moved (separately) to New York that they realized they shared an obsession with the rigors and tenets of modernism and a determination to push beyond its familiar tropes. Coincidentally, they also discovered they both have a love of vintage vehicles: Will has an Austin Healey sports car he received as compensation for his first independent design project twenty years ago; Gray has a 1947 Chris Craft motorboat that was a housewarming gift from Birmingham, Alabama, architect Bill Ingram. They are fanatical about design in all its forms.

PAGE 16
Gray Davis (left) and Will Meyer at Bowery Meat Company.

ABOVE
Gray on Copake Lake in his 1947 Chris Craft motorboat, which he had painstakingly restored.

Will and Gray also shared a career strategy: to continue their educations in New York by apprenticing with the most influential and revered architects and designers who'd hire them. After working at the Montgomery, Alabama, office of his professor Bobby McAlpine, Gray began his career in New York with the contemporary classicist John Saladino, which then led him to Thomas O'Brien's Aero Studios, where the clients included Giorgio Armani and Ralph and Ricky Lauren. Meanwhile, Will trained with two of the legendary "New York Five." He interned for the avant-garde architect Peter Eisenman and then landed a job at Gwathmey Siegel & Associates. Mentored by Charles Gwathmey, Will worked with clients such as Steven Spielberg and Michael Dell.

During these formative years, when they were becoming well versed in the principles of luxury and the whims of demanding, style-literate clients, Will and Gray would get together on weekends to discuss their more modest extracurricular projects such as an addition to Will's grandparents' weekend house in Tennessee. Eventually, they sought each other's advice when they built weekend homes for themselves. By living with their own ground-up designs, they fine-tuned their understanding of comfort, functionality, and visual impact, which are the bedrock of every project. When they founded Meyer Davis in 1999, they immediately established their practice's range by designing a trailblazing Manhattan-style nightclub in Las Vegas and a nineteenth-century-inspired farmhouse in upstate New York. Will and Gray refused to be pigeonholed. They wanted to have all kinds of clients so there would be no boundaries for their imaginations.

Will with the Austin Healey
convertible that he has owned for
more than twenty years.

Although they are fearless modernists, they are also sympathetic preservationists. Some of their most exciting projects integrate these two perspectives, blending traditional style and a cutting-edge point of view. The design equation always has a *wow* factor—high-impact moments that make an immediate and lasting impression—but there are always low-key gestures too. They believe in contrasting moods, materials, textures, and colors to create balanced—but never tame—interiors.

One of the reasons the firm has developed a global practice (with new projects underway in Sydney, Macau, and Dubai) is Will and Gray's accessibility and accountability. They are hands-on managers who have a reputation for sticking to budgets and timetables, a discipline and professionalism valued by power-player clients such as Jonathan Tisch (Loews Regency) Aby Rosen (Paramount Hotel) and Barry Sternlicht (1 Hotel South Beach). The superstar restaurateurs who've turned to them time and again include Andrew Carmellini (The Dutch in Miami Beach), John McDonald (Bowery Meat Company in Manhattan) and Ford Fry (St. Cecilia and King + Duke in Atlanta).

Their studio on the edge of SoHo is an idea incubator where an ever-expanding staff (now numbering more than sixty full-time employees) collaborates in an egalitarian environment. Will and Gray listen to everyone. They are literally at the center of the office, sketching floor plans and elevations at two conference tables surrounded by a library of books artfully arranged on shelves with objets d'art they've acquired on their extensive travels. They don't have separate offices, preferring to be in constant dialogue with each other and their project teams.

The apartments, houses, hotels, restaurants, and shops in this book are more than eye candy. They are places that are well used and well loved. Will and Gray's philosophy is straightforward: The built environment should be life affirming. Pleasure is a fundamental right. Architecture is more art than science. Good design is experiential, memorable, and uplifting.

OPPOSITE TOP

The loftlike communal area of the Meyer Davis office where Will and Gray hold meetings with their project teams.

OPPOSITE BOTTOM

The formal conference room, which is used for client presentations, has molded-plywood Eames chairs and a custom marble table.

ABOVE, RIGHT, AND BELOW

Will and Gray like to work surrounded by books and objects that fuel their imaginations.

PRIVATE

BREATHE

GRAY DAVIS AT HOME

For Gray Davis, houses only become homes when they are full of pets and people. He and his longtime partner, Chase Booth, have always had an open-door policy at their weekend retreats. The mood is completely casual. Overnight and dinner guests never have to take off their shoes. Their rule is no rules.

The houses are not fussy or precious. Gray and Chase's modus operandi when it comes to decorating is an organic, collaborative process that expresses their bond. They haunt antiques shops and second-hand stores on weekends in the Berkshires and Hudson Valley, often falling in love with woebegone pieces that they can reupholster or repaint. The furniture is sturdy, easy to maintain. The accessories are carefully edited. They repurpose furniture from one house to the next for economy, continuity, and familiarity.

As environmentalists, Gray and Chase are particularly sensitive to the landscape. They're reluctant to cut down trees, careful to maintain and protect the natural beauty of the lakefront not only for themselves but for their neighbors too. Even their motorboat—a 1947 mahogany Chris Craft fittingly named *Splinters* that took three years to restore—contributes to their curated country life.

Their preservation instincts apply to their apartment in a 1941 building with a Beaux-Arts character on a quiet lane in Greenwich Village. They searched nearly a year for a place that had not been renovated and stripped of its original details. Nevertheless, the apartment is not a time capsule. They redid the kitchen and bath, giving them a contemporary functionality and profile while winking to the past with classic materials like stainless steel, marble, and subway tiles. There are decidedly modern moments such as the semicircular banquette that follows the contour of the dining room wall and is lit by an iconic Serge Mouille light fixture.

In both the city and the country, Gray and Chase create homes for themselves—and their friends—that are comfortable, welcoming, and personal.

KNAUGHTY PINES

Copake, New York

Growing up, Gray Davis spent nearly every weekend on Center Hill Lake outside Nashville, so when he moved to New York City he planned to have a lake house of his own someday. Twenty years ago, he and Chase found a teardown on Copake Lake—except they didn't tear it down. Located two hours north of Manhattan, it was a classic 1940s bungalow that they resuscitated, modernized, and infused with a clean-cut, happy-go-lucky vibe. They painted the knotty-pine walls on the main floor a high-gloss white and ebonized the floors for a crisp, endless-summer feel. Downstairs, they reversed the coloration, with white epoxy floors and dark paneled walls creating a cozy retreat where they gravitate in winter. The outdoor spaces are as swank as lounges you'd find in a boutique hotel: a pebble-covered patio off the lower level is sheltered by jaunty all-weather curtains; the lakefront deck off the living room has a freestanding mid-century cone fireplace that Gray and Chase use in every season, wrapping themselves in blankets to stargaze on chilly nights.

PRECEDING PAGES

On the lower level of Gray's first house overlooking Copake Lake, a Grant Larkin fixture hangs above vintage 1970s chairs and a Saarinen table set on white epoxy floors,

RIGHT

The original knotty-pine walls were spray-painted white. The green bouclé "talk show" sofa and armchairs were found at an estate sale. The long-haired goatskin rug was bought in Paris.

OPPOSITE

Ikea pendant fixtures hang over a plywood table designed by Chase Booth. The chairs, found at a tag sale, have been reupholstered in white linen.

ABOVE

The house, known as Knaughty Pines, is set amid mature trees and has an appropriately rustic exterior.

RIGHT

On clear days and nights, Gray and Chase bring out a cowhide rug and leather butterfly chairs from inside to sit before the vintage Majestic fireplace on the deck overlooking Copake Lake.

OPPOSITE

Enlargements of pastoral photographs taken by a local plumber hang over a custom extra-long sofa. The support columns are wrapped in jute.

RIGHT

A pea stone–covered patio beneath the deck is an open-air lounge protected by all-weather curtains.

BELOW LEFT

The dark-stained tongue-and-groove walls and white epoxy floors on the lower level are the reverse of the living/dining room's color scheme.

BELOW RIGHT

Barn lights—used inside and outside— hang above a custom white Formica desk with mid-century chairs upholstered in cowhide.

LAKEFRONT MODERN
Copake, New York

After fourteen years in their snug cottage, Gray and Chase decided to build a masculine house that would be a more emphatic indoor/outdoor experience. A muscular combination of stucco, stained-black cedar, and brick masonry covered in vines, the house has sliding window walls on both sides of the combined kitchen, living, and dining area, so you can look straight through the front of the house to the lakeside deck, where you feel like you're floating on a barge. When the glass walls are pulled open, the interior is virtually transformed into an outdoor pavilion, and the couple find it amusing that birds fly right through the house. The elliptical chimney (inspired by Philip Johnson's cylindrical version at his landmark Glass House) serves two fireplaces—one in the living room and another on the rooftop deck, romantically landscaped with fig trees and pots of lush tropical plants. Gray and Chase incorporated many of the furnishings and fixtures from their previous home, mixing antiques and modern pieces that mingle as effortlessly as they do with their neighbors on the lake. The house has a very calming spirit, and they planned to own it forever. But when they were approached with an offer too good to turn down, they bought another piece of land on the same lake to build a more traditional house that would be a new creative challenge.

LEFT
A black cedar bulkhead box opens to the roof deck, which has a Brazilian wood floor. The pots of tropical plants are stored in the heated garage during the winter.

ABOVE

The oval chimney serves not only the roof-deck fireplace but also the one in the living room. The deck furniture, from Restoration Hardware, has custom Sunbrella upholstery.

OPPOSITE

The Grant Larkin fixture from Gray and Chase's previous house hangs in the landing that leads to the roof deck and overlooks the main living area.

TOP

A zebra hide left over from an upholstery project was framed as a piece of art in a guest room with floor-to-ceiling sliding glass doors.

ABOVE

Chase sewed the curtains out of cream burlap linen for the master bedroom, which is painted Benjamin Moore's Revere Pewter, as are all the walls in the house.

Custom floor-to-ceiling glass doors on both ends of the living room allow it to become an indoor/outdoor room. The fireplace is clad in painted brick.

ABOVE RIGHT
A classic Isamu Noguchi paper lantern
hangs above a rustic farm table. The liquor
cabinet is nicknamed "the barmoire."

RIGHT
The backsplash and island in the open
kitchen are made of Calacatta Gold marble;
the barstools have tractor-style seats

ISLAND HOUSE
Copake, New York

Although they are modernists at heart, when Gray and Chase bought property on an island in Copake Lake, they felt compelled to build a house sympathetic to the woodsy setting. Inspired by the rustic architectural style of the Adirondack Great Camps, Gray designed a contemporary interpretation of a classic lodge with steeply pitched cedar-shake roofs punctuated by shed dormers. Like their previous homes, the center of the house has a kitchen open to the combined living/dining room, which has a wall of French doors leading to a deck with a panoramic view of the lake. Grounded by a monumental interior stone wall incorporating the fireplace and a niche for wood storage, the great room has Jacobean-stained paneled walls and whitewashed pine ceilings. The thoughtful mix of vintage and contemporary furnishings expresses their appreciation for good design of any period and provenance. By tweaking a traditional vernacular and integrating a modern point of view, Gray and Chase created a house that is rustic, rugged, and refined.

A television is hidden by a sliding barn-style door on the stone wall that dominates the paneled living room.

LEFT

Vintage antlers are mounted on a paneled wall like pieces of sculpture.

OPPOSITE TOP

The whitewashed pine ceiling contributes to the rustic feeling, and transom windows with divided lights add a traditional touch to the newly built house.

OPPOSITE BOTTOM

The exterior is painted Benjamin Moore's River Rock so the house seems to blend into the wooded site.

Gray designed the custom, linen-upholstered armchair, which sits in front of the "barmoire" from their previous lake house.

RIGHT

The northern pike in a display case over the soaking tub is an exquisite example of Victorian taxidermy. The barley twist chair is upholstered in linen, and the rug is an Indian dhurrie.

BELOW

The nineteenth-century cannonball bed belonged to Gray's grandfather. The first-floor master suite opens onto the deck that runs the length of the house overlooking the lake.

WEST VILLAGE APARTMENT

New York City

Gray and Chase chose an apartment in a mid-century Greenwich Village building because it had some intact prewar character that they could tailor to their masculine sensibility. They meticulously renovated and decorated their home in a manner that gives it the cultivated air of an updated gentlemen's club. Although they spend most weekends with houseguests in the country, they like to entertain in the city too, so they furnished the living room with comfy overscale pieces—two deep clubs chairs upholstered in horsehair trimmed with leather piping and a wall-length sofa that can seat six. Gray borrowed one of his favorite ideas from restaurant projects and designed a semicircular banquette that follows the contours of the dining room's curved walls. The bowed shelf behind it holds art and books, giving the space the feel of a modern library where Chase likes to work on his laptop. They wanted the walls to reflect light and gleam night and day, so they lacquered them in Farrow & Ball's Skylight, which is one of those magical blues that morph along with the seasons. Like all of their homes, the apartment has a collected quality that reflects their long history together.

The oversized club chairs are upholstered in horsehair with leather welting. The lamp reflected in the mirror is by Isamu Noguchi.

LEFT

A credenza made of bamboo serves as a bar in the sunny sitting area next to the kitchen.

BELOW

The custom sofa, upholstered in natural-colored linen, can easily seat six people. The shimmering walls are painted Farrow & Ball's Skylight.

OPPOSITE

An antique chopping block bridges the seating area and the kitchen, which has a "quilted" stainless-steel backsplash.

ABOVE LEFT

A vintage globe rests on a Lucite stand in the master bedroom. The walls are covered in Hibernian beige linen tweed by Phillip Jeffries.

ABOVE RIGHT

The bathroom has walls of midnight-blue subway tiles and a custom marble vanity with Lucite legs.

BELOW

An abstract landscape painting by Tom Borgese hangs above the headboard.

ABOVE

A Serge Mouille light fixture hangs above a Saarinen table and a custom banquette that hugs the contours of a curved wall that's original to the apartment.

ELEVATE

WILL MEYER AT HOME

Working on his own homes, Will has put theory into practice in the most personal way. It's solidified his belief that architecture is the marriage of passion and practicality, a rational expression of emotional needs and wants.

The seminal project in his philosophical journey was his weekend house on Copake Lake. He and his wife, Kerstin, fell in love with a piece of property with stunning lake and mountain views—a tabula rasa. They were young and unencumbered, free to dream and imagine a home that would define who they were as a family. Will designed a site-specific glass house that promotes togetherness while offering privacy and quietude—a balance that informs all of his residential projects.

Even in his restrained modernist design, Will's natural exuberance comes into play with more than a few moments that make you grin such as the groovy suspended fireplace by the dining table and Nanna and Jørgen Ditzel's rattan egg chair hanging in a corner of the guest room.

Will's homes reflect his charisma. They are seductive. It's impossible not to fall in love at first sight with his beach house in the Hamptons, where the swimming pool is right by the front door. As you enter the house, you are immediately drawn outdoors by a progressive view through the kitchen, dining room, and living room to an expansive back terrace overlooking the water. Clearly, the house was designed as an antidote to urban life—a country getaway where the outdoors always beckons.

Will's an idealist and a realist. His interiors are clean, contemporary, precise compositions, but they are warm, fun, family-friendly environments too.

SKY FARM

Copake, New York

It's a rite of passage for architects to build their own homes from the ground up. Will and his wife, Kerstin, had been renting a beach house in the Hamptons when Gray told them about a parcel of land near his weekend home on Copake Lake. The sloping property had a mind-blowing, picture-perfect western view of the lake and the distant Catskill Mountains. Will instinctively envisioned a long, narrow glass house that would hover over the hillside, embracing and accentuating the stunning panorama. Inspired by California's Case Study houses and East Coast examples of mid-century architecture, Will designed a residence that reduces modernism to its essence. The house is diagrammatically straightforward, with all four bedrooms located off a spine that runs the length of the house and a central living space with the openness and sweep of a loft. A flying white frame on the exterior emphasizes the rigorous geometry of the minimalist design, and a stone buttress on the deck is a sculptural element that serves both as a place to stack firewood and as a privacy screen for the master suite. Will's home is a fine-tuned machine for living that functions as an easygoing retreat.

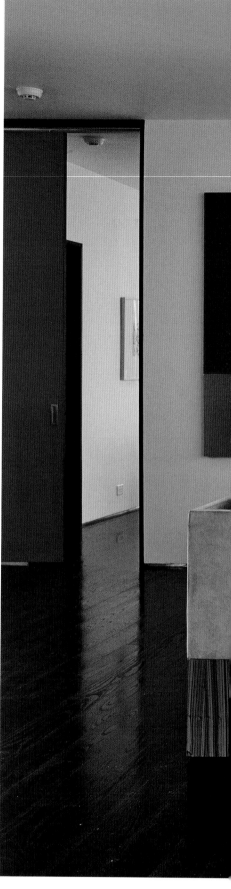

PAGES 52–53
Nestled in the woods with unobstructed views to the west, Sky Farm is cantilevered over the hillside. An open carport is hidden on the lower level.

PRECEDING PAGES

The indoor/outdoor nature of the house is emphasized by the integration of the decks and support columns into the overall design.

OPPOSITE TOP

The dining room table from Crate & Barrel is surrounded by classic Emeco Navy chairs. The light sculpture in the alcove is by John Wigmore, and the contemporary hearth is by Fireorb.

OPPOSITE BOTTOM

The kitchen, with lacquer cabinetry by Valcucine and a sleek square hood over the cooktop, is open to the living and dining area.

ABOVE

Paintings by Will's father-in-law, Enrique Battista, hang above a custom L-shaped sofa made of zebrawood with suede panels and white leather cushions.

WILLIAMSBURG TOWNHOUSE

Brooklyn, New York

When Will and Kerstin bought a newly constructed townhouse in Brooklyn's coolest neighborhood, they wanted to create an oasis for their family. In contrast to the Copake house, their primary focus was on the decor. Will approached the main living space as if it were a loft, installing a partial wall of bleached anigre that keeps the kitchen and living room distinct while allowing light to pass through the two spaces. He designed a freestanding, open bronze bookcase to divide the living and dining areas and, as he often does in public projects, used spunky overhead fixtures to define spaces: an oversized trapezoidal linen light in the living room and a knockout 1970s brass fixture in the dining area over a Saarinen table that he customized, painting the base black and adding a gray, cerused-oak top. The master bedroom is a tone poem in white, punctuated by a magnificent textured red painting by the contemporary Mexican artist Bosco Sodi. With a streamlined upholstered bed, linen curtains, and a shaggy merino wool rug, it's a restorative cocoon that allows Will and Kerstin to relax and clear their minds at the end of a typically hectic day.

ABOVE

An oil-rubbed bronze bookshelf separates the living and dining areas while keeping the public space airy and open.

RIGHT

A painting by Thilo Heinzmann, on the right, and other art from Will's collection hang above a custom sectional upholstered in gray linen. The cocktail tables are by Cassina.

ABOVE

In the dining area, a vintage 1970s brass light fixture is suspended over a Saarinen table with a gray cerused-oak top and a glossy black leather base, which is paired with Emeco chairs and a gray leather banquette.

OPPOSITE TOP

In the monochromatic master bedroom, a Le Corbusier lounge chair, upholstered in white and saddle leather, is paired with a table from Chista and a reading lamp from Flair.

OPPOSITE BOTTOM

Will designed a white linen headboard to run the length of the bedroom. The three-dimensional painting is by Bosco Sodi, and the bedside lamps are from Plug Lighting.

ABOVE

Will's son's bedroom is painted Farrow & Ball's Pavilion Gray. It is furnished with a child-sized version of Mies van der Rohe's Barcelona chair, a 1962 Arco lamp by Achille and Pier Giacomo Castiglioni, and a sconce by David Weeks.

ACCABONAC HOUSE
East Hampton, New York

The late 1960s and early 1970s were a period when the beach towns of eastern Long Island were a laboratory for hungry young architects who'd become world famous, including Will's mentor, Charles Gwathmey. When Will found an original 1971 house by the legendary Hugh Newell Jacobsen, he saw it as an opportunity to rescue an important piece of the Hamptons' pre-McMansion history. He fell in love with Jacobsen's modernist saltbox because it was perfectly sited facing Accabonac Harbor, and he was certain he could expand and update it while respecting its integrity. His strategy was to differentiate the additions—a new master suite, kitchen, and pool—with a flying white frame (similar to the one on his Copake Lake house) as a way to honor the original shingle structure. On the side facing the water, he changed the fenestration and installed new floor-to-ceiling sliding glass doors that disappear when they're open so the living room becomes an extension of the deck and vice versa. By the new courtyard entrance, wrapped in a sleek slatted fence, he built a pool that invites you to take a plunge before you step through the front door. The pas de deux between the new and old sections demonstrates Will's agility to preserve a seminal work of architecture while reinventing it.

ABOVE

A view of the rear and side elevations of the 1971 shingled saltbox by the influential architect Hugh Newell Jacobsen.

RIGHT

The living room is furnished with a sofa from B&B Italia, a coffee table by Christian Woo, a vintage chair by Milo Baughman, and a pair of Kaare Klint Safari leather chairs.

LEFT

On the far side of the living room, Will punched out a window and added a window seat that enhances Jacobsen's original design.

ABOVE

A strategically placed mirror in the living room reflects the breathtaking view of the salt marsh and bay beyond.

OPPOSITE

A lamp from Flair stands on a Herman Miller cabinet in front of a photograph by Brian Leighton.

TOP

As he often does in his restaurant projects, Will combined a banquette and chairs in the dining room, which doubles as a library.

ABOVE

A curtain embedded in the ceiling allows the dining room to be closed off from the kitchen, which overlooks the swimming pool.

TOP AND RIGHT

Will designed a slatted fence for the front of the house to give the swimming pool privacy.

ABOVE

Inspired by his work on boutique hotels, Will designed a deck with floor cushions for lounging poolside.

An expansive deck overlooking the bay is the summer dining/living room, meant for entertaining. A massive outdoor sofa beneath a mature shade tree is a sublime place to relax day or night.

CURATE

TRIBECA FLAT

New York City

Will and Gray are masters of the edit. They add and subtract with precision and finesse. Their balancing act is especially apparent when they are working with clients who collect contemporary art, and every design decision must be deferential and discerning. The owners of this apartment in a converted Tribeca warehouse hired Meyer Davis because they wanted to take a connoisseur's approach to the selection of furniture and lighting to complement their collection of bold work by artists such as Cory Arcangel, Lucien Smith, and Keltie Ferris. The clients had the patience to hunt for top-notch vintage pieces that would give their home a collected character.

Will and Gray designed some bespoke pieces to anchor the apartment. The custom dining table with seating for eight (and an extension to accommodate twelve) is surrounded by iconic teak-and-cane chairs that the Swiss architect Pierre Jeanneret designed for Chandigarh University in India; a low-slung, ten-foot-long sofa in the living room not only provides a lot of seating for parties but also allows the owners to stretch out and lounge toe-to-toe. Overhead, a museum-quality, streamlined polished-nickel picture light runs the length of the room to show the paintings to the best advantage. Will and Gray incorporated some classic furniture pieces, too, including a leather chair by the influential Brazilian modernist architect Oscar Niemeyer.

The mood is more subdued in the tone-on-tone master suite. Vintage reading lights and bedside tables by Paul McCobb flank a custom bed upholstered in luxurious Ultrasuede. Hans Wegner's oak Cow Horn chairs with leather seats are paired with a one-of-a-kind Meyer Davis desk—a floating lacquer counter topped with nickel-trimmed, parchment-faced cabinets that hide computers and the TV. It's a wholly original and finely crafted piece of furniture—a future heirloom. There is nothing ordinary in the apartment and nothing extraneous either.

ABOVE RIGHT

The gray-lacquered entry gallery features a custom shagreen table and vintage 1970s stools wrapped in zebra hide.

RIGHT

The custom kidney-shaped travertine coffee table was fabricated by Uhuru, a Brooklyn design firm.

EVERY ONE KNOWS

AND NOBODY CARES

PRECEDING PAGES

Oscar Niemeyer's 1971 Alta chair is paired with an Italian gold-leafed lamp with a high-gloss plastic shade. The walnut-and-grasscloth cabinet contains a television on a motorized lift.

OPPOSITE

A custom metal light fixture with a gold-leafed interior hangs over a custom Dean & Sylvia dining table surrounded by Chandigarh chairs by Pierre Jeanneret. The painting on the far wall is by Cory Arcangel.

ABOVE

The kitchen cabinets have nickel trim. A built-in banquette and Saarinen chairs encircle a custom Corian table with brass detailing.

OPPOSITE TOP

Hans Wegner Cow Horn chairs are paired with a custom lacquered desk. The nickel-trimmed parchment cabinets hide computers and a television.

OPPOSITE BOTTOM

In the master suite, a painting by Matthew Chambers hangs on Venetian plaster walls. The corridor of closets has the same herringbone-patterned oak floors used throughout the apartment.

ABOVE

Vintage lamps and Paul McCobb tables flank the bed, which is upholstered in Ultrasuede. The light fixture is by Serge Mouille, and the woodcut is by Andrea Büttner.

PLAY

BEACH HOUSE
Amagansett, New York

When Will and Gray's friend David Netto, the prominent interior designer, showed them the idiosyncratic 1980s house he'd bought in the Hamptons and was hell-bent on tearing down, they persuaded him to join forces on a renovation instead. Consisting of three hexagonal volumes nestled into the dunes, the house intrigued Will and Gray. They believed the original architect had a good idea but his execution was flawed, and they were determined to puzzle out a solution.

Everyone agreed that the revamped house should feel underdesigned—a celebration and elevation of the casual. The collaboration was a design ménage à trois—intense, passionate, and fun. The triumvirate ripped down interior walls and punched out new windows that breathed light into the house without altering the ecologically sensitive footprint. They replaced acres of sheetrock with horizontal paneling that looks as if it had been bleached by the sun over decades.

The uppermost hexagon was gutted and transformed into a loftlike master suite, an open space that incorporates both the sleeping and the bathing areas. The bed floats in the center of the room, its headboard doubling as one side of freestanding wood-and-glass rooms-within-a-room containing the toilet and tiled stall shower. While standing under the rainwater showerhead, David and his wife, Elizabeth, have a 360-degree view through the bedroom windows to the ocean and adjacent nature preserve.

The kitchen and main living area are loftlike too. A central structural pole supports the six-sided ceiling as if it were a tent, which is fitting because this hexagon is a bit of a three-ring circus. It has two walls devoted to cooking; a central dining area with two tables that can seat a crowd; and a lounge by the freestanding stucco fireplace set in front of a breathtakingly large plate-glass window.

Now the hexagons fulfill their potential, offering different perspectives on the landscape and flooding the house with light from all directions. Will and Gray have the satisfaction of being right, and the Nettos have the pleasure of a unique beach house that reflects their aesthetic spirit.

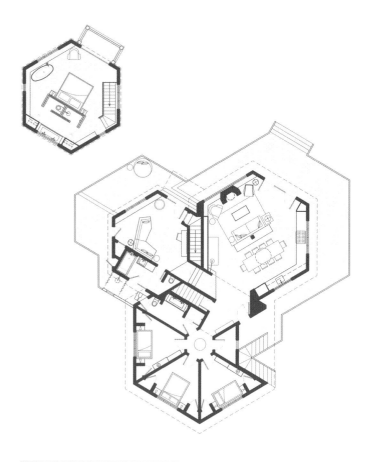

PRECEDING PAGES

The eyebrow window, French doors, and plate-glass window behind the fireplace are all additions to one of the original hexagons, which was gutted to become an open living, dining, and cooking space.

LEFT

Will and Gray collaborated with owner and interior designer David Netto not only on the architecture but also on the furniture plans.

BELOW

Two Parsons dining tables are paired with vintage leather chairs by Mario Bellini and wicker chairs by Børge Mogensen. The support column is wrapped in jute rope.

OPPOSITE

A Finn Juhl Pelican chair is a sculptural presence in front of lacquered bookcases with whitewashed white oak shelves and drawer fronts. The St. James sconce is from Ann-Morris.

OPPOSITE

Throughout the house, the floors are white oak, and the tongue-and-groove paneling is whitewashed Douglas fir, which looks as if it were faded by decades of sunlight.

ABOVE

In the family room, a custom sofa resolves the problem of furnishing an irregular space.

TOP AND ABOVE

The open bathroom has a freestanding shower that backs the headboard and a Wetstyle sink on a floating counter made of Nero Marquina marble. The leather-framed mirror is by BDDW.

RIGHT

Both the custom bed and the tub by Blu Bathworks have spectacular ocean views. The Louis XV fauteuil, upholstered in black Edelman leather, belonged to David Netto's parents.

LEFT AND RIGHT
The renovation of the house included adding and enlarging windows but maintaining the original footprint.

BELOW
Nestled into the dunes overlooking
the Atlantic Ocean, the house now has
enviable views from every room and angle.

DREAM

WEST VILLAGE TOWNHOUSE
New York City

In theory, this nineteenth-century stable and factory had been brilliantly renovated by a previous owner who carved out an enormous central atrium on the third and fourth floors with a retractable glass roof that opens to the sky. In reality, the building (previously owned by the fashion designer Richard Tyler, who used it as his atelier) was impractical for the young family who wanted to make it their permanent residence. Meyer Davis took on this logistical nightmare, determined to turn it into a dream home.

This was a project not about subtlety but about intensifying the mind-blowing architectural momentum they inherited. Every move Will and Gray made was gutsy. They designed a winding, white-lacquered staircase that leads from the reconfigured ground-floor kitchen and family room to the atrium. With its back turned to the front door, the freestanding staircase looks like an abstract piece of sculpture from the entrance and allows the family to go up and down the staircase while being shielded from the street.

The wow factor here is exponential. The enormous skylight over the kitchen and family rooms turns out to be the atrium's floor, made from a giant piece of glass—the kind of audacious gesture you'd find in an Apple store. The atrium is bookended by the living room and lower level of the duplex master bath. In the former, the clients commissioned an eye-popping, site-specific mud painting by British artist Richard Long. In the latter, glass doors open to reveal an organically shaped freestanding tub that reads as a fountain—the idea was that the bathroom could be open to the atrium without seeming indiscreet. The most surprising feature is the most inconspicuous—an outdoor shower off the top-floor master suite. Surrounded by a jungle of lush plantings, it's probably the only one of its kind in Manhattan.

Throughout, the furniture selections are eclectic—from a white Chesterfield sofa and purple-felt pool table to a live-edge dining table. The house doesn't feel in the least bit "done," just passionately collected.

PRECEDING PAGES

The atrium's glass roof is retractable, so Meyer Davis specified stucco walls and travertine floors, which are impervious to the weather.

RIGHT

A rendering reveals a clear view of the reconfigured interior that is only partially visible from the street, where the brick façade shields most of the new glass curtain wall.

BELOW

The nineteenth-century Romanesque "ruin" façade was pointed and restored with bricks of the same size and color as the originals.

OPPOSITE

The high-gloss lacquer staircase, with walnut treads and risers, reads like a piece of sculpture from the street. It's positioned so the owners can go up and down the stairs with relative privacy.

OVERLEAF

In the living room, the view to the street is framed by the brick "ruin" façade. A site-specific Richard Long painting hangs over the ethanol-fueled limestone fireplace. A contemporary Chesterfield sofa is paired with a burl wood coffee table with Lucite legs.

OPPOSITE TOP

The master bedroom, which overlooks the atrium, is adjacent to lushly planted terraces.

OPPOSITE BOTTOM

Furnished with B&B Italia outdoor furniture, the atrium is fully functional whether the glass roof is open or closed.

ABOVE

Meyer Davis designed a private outdoor shower adjacent to the master bath's glass mosaic shower.

RIGHT

The frosted-glass floor in the atrium doubles as a skylight for the kitchen, dining room, and family room.

OPPOSITE TOP

The bar in the family room has glass-and-blackened-steel doors and rift-sawn oak cabinets, which are also used beneath the counters in the kitchen.

OPPOSITE BOTTOM

The upper kitchen cabinets are half bronze and half back-painted glass. The bar stools at the island behind the sofa create a "stadium seating" plan for watching television and movies.

ABOVE LEFT

A custom Murano-glass chandelier hangs above the custom dining table, made from a slab of walnut with live edges.

ABOVE RIGHT

A leather-lined alcove provides seating in the billiards room, which has the party vibe of a lounge in one of Meyer Davis's hotel projects.

PRIVATE

LAYER

UPTOWN HOME

New York City

Will and Gray get inspired working for clients who have a strong sense of their own style. They are eternal students who learned a lot about layering art into interiors when they were engaged to renovate a classic New York townhouse for Jamie and Harold Stream, collectors of European antiques and contemporary paintings, photographs, and sculpture.

They preserved the bones of the house, but a few crucial moves—a new winding plaster staircase, for instance—give it a refreshing modern attitude. They created a clean envelope to showcase as much of the owner's eclectic collection as possible: a ceiling-high figurative sculpture by Thomas Houseago is strategically placed against a mirrored wall in the dead space of a stair landing so it can be viewed in its entirety; a four-panel gunpowder drawing by Cai Guo-Qiang is hung on a wall covered in a lush gray flannel that matches the living room sofa's upholstery. The mantra on this project: *More is more.*

But less is more too, and the designers reversed course in the kitchen, which they made a minimalist installation space like you'd find in a Chelsea gallery. The centerpiece is a long onyx island that reads like a piece of conceptual sculpture. The refrigerator and other appliances are completely hidden behind sliding lacquered panels that intentionally mirror photographer Sam Taylor-Johnson's subversive variation on Leonardo da Vinci's *The Last Supper.*

The master bath is an installation too. As if it were a diorama of a twenty-first-century home spa, it's situated behind a glass wall (with a retractable privacy scrim) on the top-floor stair landing. It has a free-standing tub beneath an enormous skylight, and the two sinks are set into a backlit, monolithic piece of Bianco Lasa marble that floats off a wall covered with a cheeky shattered-mirror veneer. Beneath the streamlined vanity, Will and Gray placed two antique giltwood benches, which they upholstered in voluptuous flokatis—a luxurious and whimsical touch that epitomizes the quirky spirit of the house.

PREEDING PAGES

The living room is a heady mix of antique French chairs, a polished-brass coffee table by Chista, a sculpture by Jonathan Meese, and a painting by Aaron Young.

LEFT

A painting by Francesco Clemente hangs over a modern mantel flanked by antique French chairs from the client's family.

BELOW

A four-panel gunpowder drawing by Cai Guo-Qiang hangs on a wall covered in a lush gray flannel. The round swivel chair is upholstered in white sable.

ABOVE

Meyer Davis designed a new staircase to
give the house a modern twist. A mirrored
wall in the landing provides a 360-degree
view of a sculpture by Thomas Houseago.

OPPOSITE TOP LEFT

A bright hallway is a segue from the master bedroom to the master study.

OPPOSITE TOP RIGHT

An antique French commode stands on the stained-concrete floor next to the staircase's sensuously curved plaster railing.

OPPOSITE BOTTOM

The master bath is set at the top of a stair landing behind a wall of glass with a retractable scrim embedded in the ceiling for privacy. It is illuminated by a skylight.

ABOVE

A long onyx island is the centerpiece of the kitchen, which has a wall of lacquered panels hiding appliances and reflecting an enormous photograph by Sam Taylor-Johnson on the opposite wall.

INSPIRE

SOHO LOFT

New York City

When Jenna Lyons, the president and creative director of J. Crew, bought a vast loft in a nineteenth-century cast-iron building in the heart of SoHo, she enlisted Meyer Davis to transform the open space into a proper apartment that would braid together varied sensibilities: uptown and downtown; bohemian and traditional; European and American. Will and Gray gave the loft new bones that evoke Paris's 16th Arrondissement—plaster walls with picture-frame moldings painted a chic pale gray, paneled solid-wood doors with brass hardware, and chevron-patterned floors made from a nuanced combination of new and reclaimed wood.

Lyons's goal was to create a home that reflected her recherché point of view. She wanted it to be child-friendly and layered with elements that provide a sense of history but with a cheeky, cutting-edge attitude. Although there's no fireplace, she decided that an antique marble mantelpiece should be the focal point of the living room as a subliminal (and sentimental) nod to Christmas Eve visits from Santa. She was determined to use materials with "deep integrity" that would develop a patina and get better with age: unlacquered brass for the counter and backsplash in the kitchen; an island with a three-inch-thick marble top for cooking and dining; unvarnished wood floors that would get beat up and leave an indelible mark of her family's life in this home.

Lyons's passion for fashion is manifest in her spectacular dressing room, a salon-like antechamber for the master bedroom that is as beautifully appointed as any boutique on the Avenue Montaigne. Her clothes hang on brass racks based on those in an old French department store, and her shoes are lined up on graduated shelves corresponding to heel heights. Lyons wanted a marble bathroom with brass fittings that would defy conventional notions of "fancy" while still being over-the-top. Will and Gray's clean, elegant composition required painstaking execution by the Meyer Davis team to book-match the purple-veined Calacatta Paonazzo marble slabs. Viewed from the raw oak–paneled bedroom through steel-and-restoration-glass doors, the bathroom appears as a sybaritic dreamscape rendered in watercolors.

PRECEDING PAGES
New walls with picture-frame moldings and an antique marble mantelpiece give the loft the feel of a nineteenth-century Paris apartment. The console table with oxidized brass legs is by Dimorestudio in Milan.

OPPOSITE

Lyons wanted the hallway to have gravitas with tall, heavyweight doors. The moldings were painted the same matte green as the walls and ceiling to give the architecture a restrained grandeur.

ABOVE

Lyons was determined to find a three-inch-thick slab of marble for the kitchen island. The counters and backsplash are made of brass that she had dipped in salt water to hasten the development of a patina. The cabinets are painted anthracite to match the La Cornue range.

OVERLEAF

Marble with purple veining was carefully book-matched for the walls, vanities, shower (on the left), and bathtub (on the right). As a counterpoint to the "fanciness" of the marble, Lyons wanted the bathroom to have the same unvarnished, chevron-patterned wood floors that Meyer Davis designed for the rest of the apartment.

ABOVE

An initial rendering of the restoration-glass doors that not only separate the sleeping and bathing areas of the master suite but also allow light from the window over the tub to filter into the bedroom.

OPPOSITE

Brass fixtures include custom medicine cabinets. The vintage sconces are by Charlotte Perriand.

OPPOSITE

Lyons's closets are meticulously made to measure with shelves for shoes of specific heel heights. Open sliding drawers hold sweaters beneath double brass racks inspired by those in an old French department store.

ABOVE

A photograph from Candida Höfer's series on great libraries hangs on the raw oak-paneled wall behind the bed. The custom brass night tables pay homage to the pioneering minimalist sculptor Donald Judd, who lived and worked in the same SoHo neighborhood.

PRIVATE

GATHER

FARMHOUSE

Tennessee

Longtime friends of Will and Gray's who'd admired their contemporary houses on Copake Lake commissioned them to build a hunting camp and weekend retreat outside Nashville that would be a gathering place for family and friends. The sprawling, secluded landscape of rolling meadows and old-growth trees lent itself to a glass house that borrows from the vernacular of mid-century modernism but has a warmth, playfulness, and practicality that distinguishes it from Miesian-style predecessors.

Will and Gray's plan is diagrammatically simple and functional. The house is shaped like a cross, with the kitchen as its literal and figurative core, so everyone naturally converges there. The kitchen is flanked by the master suite and three-bedroom guest wing on one axis and by the children's bedrooms and the two-story great room on the other—a layout that makes for easy circulation, creates distinct zones, and provides an instinctive understanding of how to experience the public and private spaces.

Will and Gray's version of modernism relies on more than steel and glass. This house is a discourse on the use of strong materials—Tennessee fieldstone for the foundation and walls, chiseled limestone for the chimneys, Douglas fir floorboards, and silvered cedar siding that was pre-aged in the fields so the exterior wouldn't weather unevenly on different elevations. These materials speak to each other indoors and outdoors, creating a cohesive aesthetic from every angle. This dialogue is reiterated by the way the couple's striking contemporary art collection has been hung so that it can be viewed from inside and outside the house; indeed, the guest wing's glass corridor is a museum-worthy gallery that's especially stunning when seen from the driveway. And because Will and Gray were building from the ground up, their furniture and lighting plan is precisely scaled to every room and its purposes—a medley of distinctive pieces (by artisans and designers such as Richard Wrightman, Lindsey Adelman, and John Wigmore) that relate to one another like guests bantering at a quick-witted dinner party.

The house is unconventional for rural Tennessee, but it's grounded in the landscape and has an organic relationship to its surroundings. Undeniably sophisticated for a "farmhouse," it has the spirit of a family compound.

PAGES 124–25

There's no need to draw the curtains at night in the double-height great room because the secluded farm has no neighbors.

PRECEDING PAGES

Custom blackened-steel-and-canvas fixtures illuminate the great room's main furniture group. A massive two-tiered wood coffee table is flanked by a Poliform sectional and a Christian Liaigre sofa.

OPPOSITE

The solid wood front doors open directly into the dining area of the great room, where a custom Lindsey Adelman chandelier hangs above a local walnut slab table surrounded by Richard Wrightman chairs.

RIGHT

The kitchen has cerused-oak cabinets and Gris Pulpis marble countertops. Two prep islands allow several people to cook simultaneously.

BELOW

A third island doubles as a divider between the kitchen and the great room.

PRECEDING PAGES

The master suite is its own wing. Custom sliding glass walls provide access to a private terrace.

OPPOSITE

The Isola daybed by Jeff Vioski for Suite NY is designed for two; it's paired with Angelo Brotto's sculptural Giraffe lamp from the 1970s.

RIGHT

The corner window walls open to the outdoors for alfresco bathing in the Agape tub.

FAR RIGHT

A view from the shower in a guest room to the floating vanity set against a wall of glass; a motorized bottom-up shade offers privacy.

BELOW

Richard Avedon's photograph of Nastassja Kinski hangs on the wall-sized hide headboard. The bedside lamps, by Ingo Maurer, are made of crinkled Japanese paper.

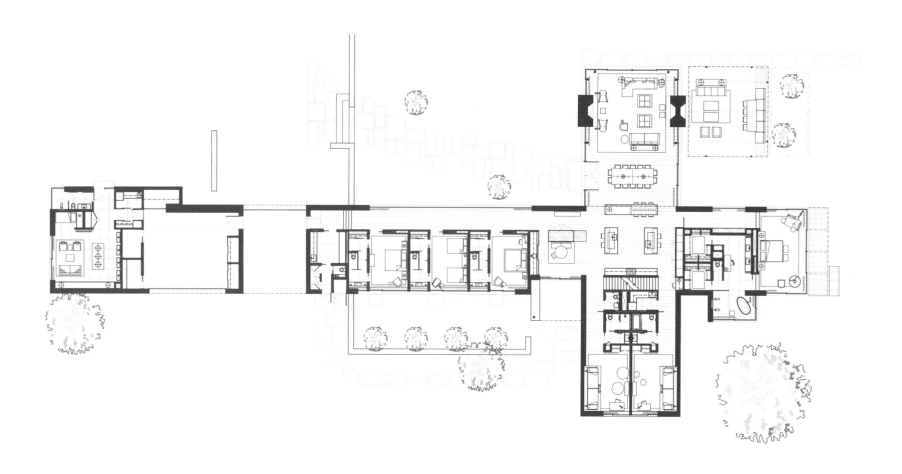

ABOVE

The house is designed like a cross with the kitchen as the nexus; the master suite and guest rooms are on the east-west axis, and the great room and children's bedrooms are on the north-south axis.

LEFT

The pergola and terrace are integrated into the design of the house to create an outdoor extension of the great room.

BELOW

The profile of the house is deliberately restrained to respect the surrounding landscape.

OPPOSITE

The pergola is covered with tensile fabric that lets light penetrate but not rain. The fireplace shares a chimney with one in the great room. The teak table is a custom design and the chairs are from Sutherland.

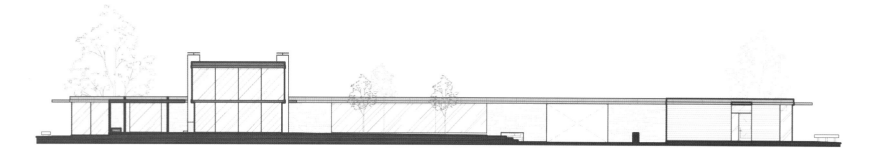

IMAGINE

UPPER EAST SIDE TOWNHOUSE
New York City

In the popular imagination, New York is a city of high-rise living—from the limestone apartment buildings on Fifth and Park Avenues to the glass towers that increasingly dominate the downtown skyline. But New York is also a city rife with single-family homes, and none are more majestic than the late nineteenth- and early twentieth-century mansions that line the side streets of the Upper East Side.

Meyer Davis was commissioned to design a seven-level house that would be compatible with its landmarked neighbors on one of the toniest blocks near the Metropolitan Museum of Art. The site had once held two undistinguished townhouses that had been ingloriously combined into a small apartment building, so there were no qualms about demolishing it, which gave Will and Gray a 32-foot-wide double lot for building a 14,000-square-foot residence with seven bedrooms and eight bathrooms.

The clients imagined the new house as an old mansion—dignified, stately, imposing—that would appear to have been thoughtfully and immaculately renovated: Old World details preserved and reinterpreted by a strict minimalist with sophistication and a sense of whimsy. Will and Gray's challenge was to synthesize the clients' wish list, editing and re-editing the floor plans and finishes as choices were made about artwork and furnishings. Their masterstroke was adding ultra-contemporary "insertions," such as the kitchen and reading room, which are both counterpoints and complements to the traditional architecture.

The rigor of the collaboration with the clients yielded stunning results. White porcelain lily of the valley tendrils seem to organically emerge from the plaster wall that runs along the staircase from the first to the second floors. The blazingly white spaces have depth, warmth, and texture because they were painstakingly hand-brushed in multiple layers by master artisans. Intentional gaps between some of the boards in the herringbone-patterned, patinated oak floors contribute to the illusion that this is actually a historic mansion. By crossing classical and avant-garde sensibilities, Will and Gray created a house that is ethereal and sublime.

PRECEDING PAGES

The wall connecting the first and second floors is ornamented with a tangle of porcelain lilies of the valley by Los Angeles artist David Wiseman.

ABOVE

Inspired by nineteenth-century mansions in London, Paris, and Manhattan, Meyer Davis designed a limestone façade with classic details for the seven-story house.

OPPOSITE TOP

The entry foyer has Bleu de Savoie marble floors with borders of Bianco Puro marble, which was also used in the kitchen. The bronze sconces are by Wever & Ducré, and the table is by French designer Nathan Litera.

OPPOSITE BOTTOM

The husband's reading and relaxation room is entirely upholstered in Ultrasuede with hidden cabinets for books and an oculus in the ceiling to bring in light.

TOP

Vintage mid-century chairs from the Paris flea market surround a table by Nathan Litera in the dining area, which is open to the kitchen.

ABOVE

Floor-to-ceiling pocket doors allow the kitchen to be closed off from the dining area.

OPPOSITE

The minimalist kitchen has marble counters, lacquer cabinets, and a Black Cherry Twin Lamp, Gold Edition, by Nika Zupanc.

PPRECEDING PAGES

The client and contractor collaborated on the installation of Mathieu Lehanneur's Les Cordes chandelier. Made of glass tubes and LED lights, it looks like ropes hanging down from the ceiling. The painting is by Henning Strassburger.

OPPOSITE TOP

The design of the staircase created an atrium connecting the foyer and living room.

OPPOSITE BOTTOM LEFT

The sensuous modern curves of the staircase are in sharp contrast to the traditional architectural details.

OPPOSITE BOTTOM RIGHT

Vintage Fritz Hansen high-back armchairs upholstered in sheepskin can be used in either of the living room's two furniture groups.

RIGHT

A neon sculpture by Tracey Emin hangs in the corridor connecting the living room and library.

ABOVE

Niamh Barry's Apparent Magnitude, a bronze light fixture, hangs in the walnut-paneled library, which was designed so it could be converted into a formal dining room if necessary.

OPPOSITE

The vintage Harvey Probber sectional sofa, upholstered in crushed velvet, has a polished-chrome base that reflects the gray wood floors. A curved surface painting by Ron Gorchov hangs over the sofa.

PUBLIC

COLLECT

ST. CECILIA

Atlanta

Will and Gray are thoughtful interpreters of their clients' dreams. They have a talent for tapping into other people's ambitions and transmogrifying them into three dimensions. They were tuned into star chef Ford Fry's vision for his third restaurant, which would have a menu focusing on seafood and the flavors of the Italian coast. He wanted the restaurant to look like it was built on memories of a chef's journey through Italy—the postcards, matchbooks, coasters, train stubs, and other ephemera that he collected along the way. This scrapbook became Will and Gray's inspiration for St. Cecilia, a collage of artifacts and honest materials (reclaimed wood, leather, brass, steel, ceramic tiles) that they deftly combined so diners feel like they're on a journey too.

Diners at St. Cecilia have a sense of wonder when they arrive at the reception desk, which is set in front of a colossal brass-and-oak bookcase filled with collections of quirky antiques, books, bottles, and taxidermy. As they descend the staircase to the main dining room, guests have an *Aha!* moment when they realize that the bookcase is the back of the monumental racetrack bar that grounds the vast, high-ceilinged restaurant. It may register only subconsciously, but it's telling that the curtains draping the window wall are a patchwork of sturdy canvases stitched together with twine as if made by fishermen's wives from old sailcloth. Meyer Davis employed its trademark recipe for making guests feel cozily embraced in a large restaurant, creating zones defined by a spectrum of pendant lights and different seating options such as the knockout round banquettes that float in the center of the restaurant.

That Will and Gray approached St. Cecilia as if they were set designers makes sense because the space is as vast as a soundstage. And what's made St. Cecilia's so successful is the marriage between the cuisine and the décor, an immersive experience in which it's possible to feel like you're in a remake of *La Dolce Vita*.

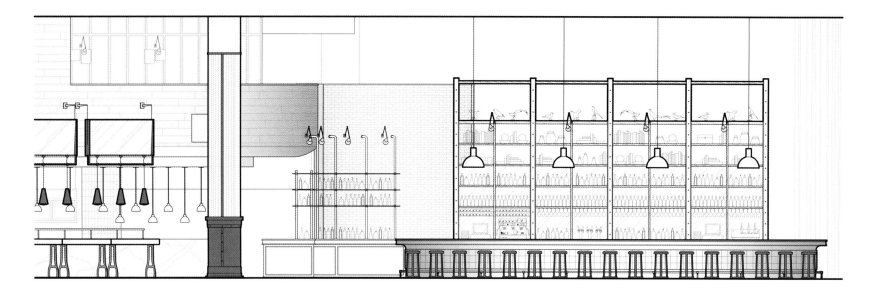

PRECEDING PAGES

The upper half of the monumental bookcase behind the bar is open to offer a view into the restaurant from the reception desk on the other side. Backless barstools allow patrons to drink facing the dining room.

ABOVE

The rendering shows how library and pendant lights are used to delineate various sections of the restaurant.

BELOW

St. Cecilia is divided into several zones, including a lounge area with a sectional upholstered in fabric and leather.

OPPOSITE

A collection of books and artifacts alludes to a chef's journey along the Mediterranean coast, which was inspiration for the restaurant.

LEFT

The central zone of the dining room has floating, easy-to-access circular banquettes with two-tone leather backs.

ABOVE

A view of the open kitchen through the raw bar, with shelves holding Italian groceries.

ABOVE

The repetition of circular forms in the furniture and lighting gives cohesion to the restaurant's design.

OPPOSITE TOP LEFT

Reclaimed-wood floors provide a rustic counterpoint to the restaurant's sleek chairs and banquettes.

OPPOSITE TOP RIGHT

A patchwork of canvas, the curtains are meant to seem as if they were sewn out of sails from old fishing boats. The leather-strapped chairs are from Mexico.

OPPOSITE BOTTOM LEFT

Midnight-blue leather banquettes for more intimate dining are bordered by light strips; the mirrors above add shimmer and reflection.

OPPOSITE BOTTOM RIGHT

Industrial light fixtures and columns sheathed in white subway tiles and blackened steel suggest the waiting room of an Italian train station.

PUBLIC

DAZZLE

PARAMOUNT HOTEL

New York City

Constructed just steps from Times Square in 1928 by celebrated movie palace architect Thomas W. Lamb, the 600-room Paramount was relaunched by Ian Schrager as a boutique hotel in 1990 with an avant-garde design by Philippe Starck. After two decades, however, Starck's trendsetting interiors had been tweaked beyond recognition, and new owner Aby Rosen hired Meyer Davis to make the hotel hip, relevant, and cutting edge again.

The Paramount's landmarked French Renaissance façade and flamboyant history as the home of Billy Rose's legendary Diamond Horseshoe nightclub guided Will and Gray's creative process. They reimagined the hotel as a mash-up of theater motifs—borrowed from the hundreds of fantastical movie houses designed by Lamb—reinterpreted for contemporary cocktail culture.

The design of the two-story lobby was the core of the project because of its vast size and need to function as a grand salon where guests hang out and socialize around the clock. The lobby relates and responds to its Times Square location: it's in sync with the neighborhood's sexy, up-all-night vibe and, paradoxically, it's a relaxing retreat for hotel guests to escape the hullabaloo outside the front door.

The transition from the street is dramatic. Guests pass through a bright vestibule into a kaleidoscopic two-story atrium with dark oak walls and a show-stopping stainless-steel fireplace that reflects the light and energy of the room. Dominated by a thirty-foot-long leather daybed for lounging and a groovy eight-seat cloverleaf-shaped upholstered banquette sheathed in stainless steel, the asymmetrical furniture plan is at once playful and cozy, humanizing the vast space while maximizing its seating capacity. References to Broadway architecture include armchairs upholstered in vibrant velvets like those found on the seats at nearby theaters and stage lights suspended from the ceiling. On the mezzanine, a DJ booth and lounge area offer a bird's-eye view of one of the best shows in town.

PRECEDING PAGES

A deejay booth perched over the fireplace and a lacquered ceiling that reflects the room's activity contribute to the two-story lobby's nightclub ambience.

TOP

The lobby's furniture plan is a mix of seating groups that maximize its capacity.

ABOVE

A custom cloverleaf-shaped banquette clad in stainless steel is upholstered in luxurious velvet.

RIGHT

The focal point of the lobby is the stainless-steel fireplace, which was designed to reflect the light and energy of the room.

LEFT

A plaster bust on the concierge desk is an unexpected and welcome classical touch in the contemporary space.

BELOW

A view through the installation of Coltrane Pipe Pendant lights that contribute to the lobby's jazzy Times Square ambience.

OPPOSITE

A thirty-foot-long ottoman has an assortment of throw pillows to encourage guests to make themselves at home in the lobby.

OVERLEAF

The chevron pattern on the floor of the restaurant is echoed in the leather base of the zinc-topped bar.

OPPOSITE

Against a white brick wall, the mirrored wine shelves trimmed in brass reiterate the chevron motif in a subtle and functional manner.

RIGHT

The artwork in the restaurant's lounge includes Broadway memorabilia that references the Paramount's location in the heart of the theater district.

BELOW

Mirrors throughout the restaurant create vistas that help disguise the fact that the space has no windows.

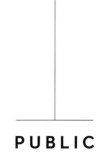

DELIGHT

OSCAR DE LA RENTA BOUTIQUES

New York City | Los Angeles | London

The late fashion designer Oscar de la Renta was a dream client. Long known for dressing socialites and political figures (including Nancy Reagan, Barbara Bush, and Hillary Clinton), Oscar was also a favorite of actresses (such as Sarah Jessica Parker, Kristen Stewart, and Tina Fey) who made him the master of the red carpet. He hired Meyer Davis to design stores that would bridge the generations and reflect his esteemed brand's evolution and modernity.

Inspired by the vernacular of the beachfront home Oscar built for himself at Punta Cana in his native Dominican Republic, Will and Gray decided that the materials used for his villa—coquina, plaster, lacquer, bleached wood—could become the building blocks for flagship shops (as well as department-store boutiques) that would be both contemporary and timeless. As a backdrop for his ornate and beautifully detailed clothing, the retail environment had to be clean, airy, and understated.

Will and Gray established a unique visual vocabulary for the stores— a toolkit of elements that could be combined in different configurations so that each boutique would embrace its locale and have a unique personality while staying true to the brand. In London, for instance, they worked in a listed Edwardian townhouse on Mount Street in Mayfair, where historic regulations limited the architectural changes they could make. They incorporated an existing fireplace and rococo staircase by painting them white so they whisper. On the façade of the Manhattan flagship on Madison Avenue, they trimmed the plate-glass windows with limestone to correspond with the architectural details of the prewar apartment building above it. And on Melrose Place in Los Angeles, they transformed a carriage house with a private garden into a shopping oasis with a luxurious, laid-back West Coast vibe.

So far, Meyer Davis has built fifteen Oscar de la Renta boutiques (and fifteen shop-in-shops for department stores) around the world. Each one is a sublime showcase for clothes and accessories that transcends fashion. The stores epitomize the impeccable style and taste of the late designer, who was a paragon of the well-lived life.

PRECEDING PAGES

A brick path leads to the entrance of the Melrose Place flagship, where a pot of orchids atop a stone table creates a gracious, residential-style welcome.

OPPOSITE TOP

A long, narrow video screen is inserted into a coquina wall at the Melrose Place boutique.

OPPOSITE BOTTOM LEFT

The plaster palm bas-relief is one of the couture details that give the boutiques a tinge of tropical glamour.

OPPOSITE BOTTOM RIGHT

Walls of windows at the Melrose Place boutique offer an alluring view of the merchandise.

ABOVE LEFT

A wall with floating shelves offers flexible display space for home or fashion accessories.

ABOVE RIGHT

A tiered formation of shelves offers a panorama of diverse Oscar de la Renta product lines.

BELOW

A ramp incorporated into the design of the Manhattan flagship makes the multilevel store elegantly wheelchair accessible.

LEFT

The existing wrought-iron staircase at the London store is a historic element elegantly juxtaposed with a video screen showing a loop of the latest runway show.

ABOVE LEFT

Mirrored shelves allow for easy browsing of accessories from every angle.

ABOVE RIGHT

The contrast between the London boutique's original moldings and sleek cabinetry reflects the brand's blend of tradition and modernity.

RIGHT

The shelves of the shoe salon are lit to highlight the merchandise.

ABOVE

Plaster palm trees frame the dressing rooms in a fanciful Caribbean style that harkens back to Oscar de la Renta's native Dominican Republic.

RIGHT

The original marble mantelpiece in the London store is another historic element that Meyer Davis deftly incorporated into a contemporary design scheme.

PASSION

BIRTHE OG NIELS ROKKEDALS SAMLING

VENDSYSSEL KUNSTMUSEUM
P. Nørkjærs Plads 15 · Hjørring

15. marts - 18. maj 2003 · Alle dage: 10 - 16 · Mandag lukket

CELEBRATE

THE DUTCH
Miami Beach

Will and Gray's working relationship with chef Andrew Carmellini goes back to 2009, when they designed Laconda Verde for him at Robert De Niro's Greenwich Hotel in Tribeca. It was an overnight sensation—a destination restaurant *and* a neighborhood hangout. The locals fell in love with Carmellini's impeccably sourced "family-style" Italian food. They quickly became regulars. It seemed as if Meyer Davis had designed it just for them—a warm and welcoming eatery with the feel of a chic clubhouse.

When Carmellini decided to open a restaurant called the Dutch in Miami Beach a few years later, he challenged Meyer Davis to design another neighborhood haunt. Will and Gray understood that the restaurant had to be imbued with the ethos of Miami Beach—a place where locals would feel a sense of belonging along with New Yorkers who make Miami their second home during the winter. Located in the slick and sophisticated W Hotel (which already had a glossy Mr. Chow restaurant), the Dutch was designed to be relaxed, unpretentious, irresistible—as comfortable for a breakfast of buttermilk pancakes as for a late-night supper of oysters and Champagne.

Will and Gray sheathed the walls in whitewashed brick, a timeless backdrop for bookshelves filled with beach-house paraphernalia such as model boats, game boards, and jars of shells. They designed custom wood chairs with leather cushions trimmed in brass rivets in a modernist style that pays homage to Miami Beach during its mid-century heyday. They also designed dusky blue-gray banquettes with white cushions strapped onto them like you'd find on a yacht, and continued the nautical motif by suspending mirrors, light fixtures, and the shelves behind the bar with the type of strapping used for shipping containers. Despite being a hotel restaurant, the Dutch has become exactly what Carmellini imagined—a beachy, neighborhood joint that is the quintessence of Miami Beach.

PRECEDING PAGES

Two different sets of light fixtures create a visual separation between the bar and the dining room in the front section of the restaurant. The hostess desk and bar have matching leather bases and zinc tops.

ABOVE LEFT

A wall of custom bookshelves holds souvenirs and objets d'art that contribute to the surfside Miami Beach mood.

ABOVE RIGHT

The interior entrance to the restaurant lures guests to join the scene at the bar.

OPPOSITE

The bar area is defined by trapezoidal fluted-glass light fixtures. The custom modernist-inspired barstools, upholstered in blue-gray leather, match the chairs in the dining room.

A rendering depicts how brick-clad columns were used to create virtual rooms and intimate spaces for tables for two.

ABOVE

A large hanging mirror is used to make the dining room more expansive. A giant banquette is shared by two tables that can be combined for a large party.

OPPOSITE, CLOCKWISE FROM TOP LEFT

Attention to details is a Meyer Davis hallmark: antiqued mirrors are suspended by a pulley system; a rope sculpture by Chase Booth is an abstract nautical reference; fabric cushions are strapped onto the leather banquette in a manner often found on yachts; the leather back on a custom mid-century-style chair is trimmed in brass rivets.

OVERLEAF LEFT

A large mirror and a floor-to-ceiling wine wall are striking gestures that add drama to a private dining room.

OVERLEAF RIGHT

The custom metal-mesh hanging lights in the outdoor dining room allow breezes to flow through them so they don't sway on windy days.

REVEL

THE WAYFARER

New York City

Situated in the heart of midtown Manhattan, the Wayfarer was conceived as a restaurant that would be as dynamic as its location at the kinetic intersection of 57th Street and Sixth Avenue. Meyer Davis's concept was to give it a sense of belonging to the city's past and present—an only-in-New York destination that would appeal to locals and tourists alike. Will and Gray imagined its having an eccentric history: an early twentieth-century men's club that had been turned into a pimped-out, see-and-be-seen restaurant during the disco era and left untouched for decades after it closed. As if they were archaeologists as well as architects, they wanted to salvage these virtual remains and use them as a point of departure for generating and structuring the project.

After gutting the two-story space, located in a 1929 building by Emery Roth, they installed contemporaneous paneling painted a deep flannel gray that's the ideal backdrop for a salon-style installation of pop art paintings and bold photographs. They designed supersexy serpentine banquettes upholstered in caramel-colored leather that snake through the front of the restaurant and meander along the perimeter of the second-floor bar and lounge. Accessed by a zigzagging, freestanding staircase, the lounge has a blackened-steel Moroccan-trellis screen overlooking the open stairwell, a gutsy gesture that creates a psychedelic view of more abstract and pop art hung on a shirred-fabric wall.

With windows facing the street on two sides, the Wayfarer required a layered lighting program so it would shine day and night, as the restaurant serves breakfast, lunch, and dinner. Constellations of spherical fixtures hang from the ceiling. Mammoth swing-arm lamps illuminate the tufted banquettes on the main floor's back walls, which are bordered by horizontal mirrored panels that add flash. Every element is inextricably linked, a harmonious eclecticism that has a cosmopolitan rhythm.

PRECEDING PAGES

An industrial-style swing-arm lamp illuminates a corner banquette upholstered in tweed and leather. An installation of 1970s art pays homage to the restaurant's narrative of having once been a disco-era hotspot.

ABOVE

Separated from the dining room by a low banquette, the bar attracts a lively crowd that sets the tone for the restaurant.

OPPOSITE

One of the restaurant's serpentine banquettes sits beneath the staircase leading to the second-floor lounge.

A nook for cocktails by the bar is
separated from the dining room by
atmospheric wavy glass.

ABOVE

Custom blackened-steel-framed mirrors with brass straps hang above a custom Calacatta marble counter in the men's room. The floor is covered with geometric-patterned cement tiles.

RIGHT

The 1960s sex symbol Bridget Bardot was the inspiration for the mural by Victor Fung in the corridor leading to the restrooms.

LEFT

A wall of black-and-white photographs in the upstairs bar is a time capsule that celebrates the swinging 1960s and 1970s.

TOP

A rendering of the second floor illustrates the echo between the swirl of marquee lights overhead and the serpentine banquettes.

ABOVE

In the second-floor lounge, chairs and tables are easily moved to accommodate small and large groups.

ENJOY

KING + DUKE

Atlanta

As Southerners, Will and Gray intuitively understood the concept that Atlanta chef Ford Fry had for his restaurant King + Duke, which is named after the hilarious hucksters in Mark Twain's *Adventures of Huckleberry Finn.* Serving an inventive farm-to-table menu of updated Southern comfort food, the restaurant has a design scheme in keeping with its name and a narrative that informs the dining experience.

Meyer Davis established a literary leitmotif at the rough-hewn reception desk, which is surrounded by floor-to-ceiling bookcases and a rolling library ladder—it's as if you've arrived at the home of a modern-day Faulkner. Most of the restaurant's food is cooked over wood on a twenty-four-foot-long hearth in an open kitchen that fills the restaurant with a intoxicating campfire aroma. Riffing on this olfactory sensation, the architects played with forms and materials that are rugged and outdoorsy. They designed burlap-covered seating reminiscent of campaign chairs and low-slung leather folding screens as partitions. It's as if Will and Gray mixed and matched elements from a quail shoot on a plantation and a deluxe African safari.

A feeling of comfortable chic permeates the restaurant—from the worn leather sofa in the front lounge to the banquettes with leather seats and upholstered backs. Shaded standing lamps and a mix of overhead lighting define different areas of the restaurant, which glows like charcoal embers in the evening. There are moments of intimacy amid the wide-open space to counterbalance the double-height window walls that connect to the outdoor dining decks. As with most Meyer Davis projects, the final 10 percent of the design hinged on Will and Gray's personally curating accessories and hanging a collection of art that ensures the restaurant has its own distinctive character.

To conceive and build such an easygoing and stylish restaurant requires obsessive attention to details—the whole *is* the sum of its parts. King + Duke has become an Atlanta institution because it pulses with the city's sophisticated energy while exuding good ol' Southern hospitality.

PRECEDING PAGES

The leather sectional in the lounge at the front of the restaurant is separated from the dining room by a low folding leather screen.

ABOVE LEFT

A collection of art is hung on a wall of blue subway tiles behind the hostess desk, which is made of reclaimed wood.

ABOVE RIGHT

Shelves filled with books allude to the restaurant's being named after two characters from *The Adventures of Huckleberry Finn*.

OPPOSITE

Custom brass-plated light fixtures hang over the bar, which has a marble base and a wood top. Meyer Davis designed the leather-and-iron barstools.

LEFT

The gut renovation included raising the ceiling to expose beams and adding window walls. The two-tone custom chairs have brown leather seats and fabric backs with leather straps, which make them reminiscent of folding campaign furniture.

TOP

The banquettes have blue leather seats and menswear-inspired back cushions.

ABOVE

Meyer Davis tiled the niche where most of the food is cooked over an open fire and covered the elaborate exhaust system in blackened metal.

REMEMBER

HARLOW
New York City

When the newspaper mogul William Randolph Hearst built the Lombardy Hotel in 1926, he designated a suite of ground-floor rooms for hosting parties with his paramour, the actress Marion Davies. Embellished with elaborate plaster moldings, bas-reliefs, oak paneling, interior leaded-glass windows, and crystal chandeliers, these private spaces had remained basically intact for nearly a century. Hospitality industry veteran Richie Notar (who started his career as a doorman at Studio 54 and became a managing partner for the Nobu chain) hired Meyer Davis to turn the ballroom-sized space into a lounge and restaurant called Harlow (named after the 1930s screen siren) that could also be used for special events such as movie premieres. With the goal of preserving and enhancing the majesty of the original design, Will and Gray deftly balanced restoration and innovation while layering in contemporary elements as if they were colorizing an old black-and-white movie.

From the reception desk, a jaunty striped hallway frames the view to the lounge, where ultramodern hand-blown-glass trumpet lights are centered over cocktail tables. The restored rococo archways behind the white leather bar offer views into a conservatory dining room with skylights and a luxuriant live plant wall.

The awesome view from the lounge to the 100-seat dining room culminates at the marble oyster bar, which is backed by a mirrored wall fancifully hand painted with schools of frolicking fish. The designers restored all of the original woodwork and inserted mirrors into each panel at eye level to open up the space and add sparkle. They backlit the existing leaded-glass Gothic windows, cleaned and re-hung the ornate crystal chandeliers, and designed brass light-box end tables that not only define seating areas but add a warm, romantic glow. By honoring the traditional architecture and combining it with streamlined seating and plush curved banquettes, Will and Gray gave Harlow an equipoise that makes old-style Hollywood glamour relevant to today.

PRECEDING PAGES

The oyster bar at the far end of the main dining room features a mirror hand-painted with playful schools of fish. Each seat has its own napkin rack.

OPPOSITE

The corridor leading from the reception desk to the lounge is painted with wide stripes that echo the ceiling beams.

ABOVE

In the cocktail lounge, hand-blown-glass trumpet lights by Vistosi are in striking contrast to the restored plasterwork and woodwork.

LEFT

Fontana Arte half-moon suspension lamps hang over the bar, behind which is a semiprivate dining room.

RIGHT

Custom mirrors draped with plants spread light in the conservatory dining room behind the bar.

BELOW

An early rendering of the cocktail lounge shows four half-moon pendants over the bar, but in the final design Meyer Davis used two larger pendants that echo the restored fanlights behind them.

OVERLEAF

The original backlit stained-glass windows and rock crystal chandeliers were refurbished. Light boxes with mushroom lamps add a soft light and function as discreet room dividers.

PAGE 208, CLOCKWISE FROM TOP LEFT

Mirrors were inserted into the restored paneling at eye level to make the room seem larger when one is walking through, but more intimate when one is sitting; Meyer Davis saved many original details such as the clock above the door; each place setting at the oyster bar has its own polished-chrome lamp; a silhouette of a businessman on his cell phone marks the men's room.

PAGE 209

The fish on the mirror behind the bar were hand-painted by Katherine Blackburne.

CAROUSE

BOWERY MEAT COMPANY
New York City

The great New York steak houses have always been stoked by martinis and machismo. Whether buttoned up or raucous, they tend to blur together as relics of bygone days when cigars were the ritual conclusion of red-blooded meals. Restaurateur John McDonald chose Meyer Davis to help him reinvent the steak house for one of New York's hippest downtown neighborhoods. The location, just off the Bowery—not so long ago Manhattan's skid row and now a boulevard of boutique hotels and swank shops—guided Will and Gray's back-to-the-future design. And so did chef/partner Josh Capon's maverick menu, which naturally has a roster of great cuts of beef (including the eponymous Bowery Steak) as well as unexpected dishes like duck lasagna and deviled eggs with caviar.

Bowery Meat Company feels both familiar and original. It has just enough retro elements—mid-century chairs, sleek walnut paneling, vintage factory lights—that it could have been a location for the final season of *Mad Men*, when pioneering female ad executives like Peggy Olson and Joan Harris finally felt comfortable ordering the wine and picking up the check. Bowery Meat Company could be deemed a post-feminist steak house: although it has a masculine aesthetic, it doesn't feel like an old boys' club. By design, it's embracive rather than exclusive.

The restaurant's conversation piece is the wine wall at the far end of the main dining room. It's actually a temperature-controlled wine room separated by a steel-and-glass storefront-style window. It's both decorative and functional, an artfully arranged storage facility for the restaurant's extensive wine program that casts a warm glow in the evening over the classic semicircular banquettes and the wood tables surrounded by vintage mid-century chairs.

The collaboration between Meyer Davis and McDonald is ongoing. The design has a degree of flexibility that allows the owner to rotate the artwork and add cool stuff he finds to the display case by the reception desk. Bowery Meat Company's bonhomie is a product of Will and Gray's ability to support and channel McDonald's notion of hospitality.

PAGES 210–11

A mixed medley of vintage chairs, geometric-patterned carpet and curtains, and a mural-sized painting of an airplane flying over Manhattan contribute to the restaurant's retro atmosphere.

PRECEDING PAGES

A chicken-wire-glass cabinet at the entrance is like a glowing lantern. Restored factory lights are suspended over the bar. The canoe hanging from the ceiling was repurposed from the owner's MercBar in SoHo.

LEFT

Meyer Davis's layered lighting plan in one corner includes a small table lamp, a vintage sconce from the owner's collection, and a satellite chandelier.

BELOW

None of the restaurant's fixtures or finishes is overrefined, which is in keeping with the spirit of its once gritty East Village neighborhood. In the background, a temperature-controlled wine room, separated by storefront-style windows, is both decorative and functional.

ABOVE

A combination of walnut paneling and glazed ceramic tiles gave Bowery Meat Company a patina from day one.

DINE

VAUCLUSE
New York City

Once upon a time, the white tablecloth French restaurant serving haute cuisine was the standard against which all New York restaurants were measured. Lavish and often stuffy, they were the sort of pretentious places that required men to wear jackets and ties. They are virtually extinct—the dinosaurs of fine dining. Chef Michael White, who developed his reputation with his Italian food at two Michelin-starred Manhattan restaurants, imagined reinventing the fancy French restaurant. He chose Meyer Davis to execute his vision for a Gallic gastronomic experience that was fun rather than formidable.

Will and Gray took cues from White's menu (updated versions of classics like Veal Rossini and duck à l'orange) and the posh location (Park Avenue and 63rd Street). They envisioned a clientele of movers and shakers arriving in their chauffeured Escalades and well-heeled locals who'd walk over from their splendid co-op apartments.

Vaucluse's main high-ceilinged dining room has the feel of a grand salon that's been painstakingly edited with a chic, contemporary sensibility. Anchored by a monumental central banquette with seating on four sides, the room is a mellow mélange of tradition and innovation—plasterwork ceilings, parquet floors, and paneled walls paired with a sleek suspended light fixture and elegant étagères that double as waiter stations. It's a seductive and romantic space. The *New Yorker* declared that Vaucluse has "the kindest, not to say the loveliest, lighting of any restaurant in New York."

Unlike old-school French restaurants, Vaucluse is neither haughty nor hushed. It has a central barroom that's a convivial spot for an aperitif. The bar is also a passageway to the restaurant's other dining room, which is visible though hand-rubbed, mottled-plaster archways that evoke a château in the countryside. The design is luxuriously restrained so diners focus on White's sublime cooking, expertly served by an unfailingly courteous and conscientious waitstaff. In every respect, Vaucluse is a tour de force.

PRECEDING PAGES

The center of the main dining room at Vaucluse has a long, narrow, four-sided banquette upholstered in warm gray fabric that grounds the room and maximizes the seating by minimizing the space between tables.

OPPOSITE

A three-dimensional mirror installation functions as both a piece of sculpture and a device to add depth to the room.

ABOVE

A sleek racetrack light fixture over the banquette hangs from a new tracery ceiling punctuated with three mirror-outlined, glazed-brick barrel vaults.

BELOW

A schematic for the main dining room specifies furniture in elevation with the oversize windows.

PRECEDING PAGES

In the second dining room, art pottery by Sara Paloma is reflected in the mirrored screen. The chairs on the left are an original Meyer Davis design.

LEFT

The central waiters' station was designed and lit so that the wine-glass storage would be a glittering sculptural presence in the middle of the dining room.

BELOW

The floor plan shows that the bar is the nexus of the restaurant; it is designed to complement the two differently decorated dining rooms.

OPPOSITE

A geometric-patterned carpet and an oversize linen lampshade are used to define a seating area with a table surrounded by classic Saarinen chairs.

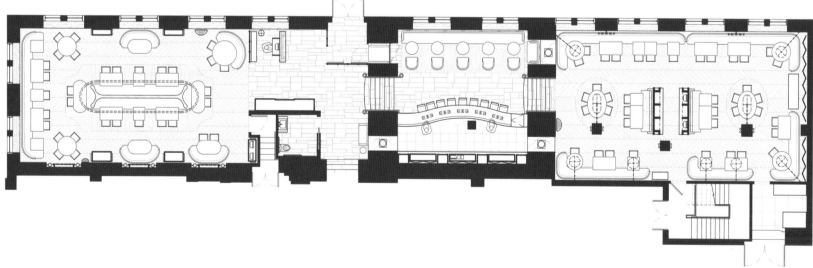

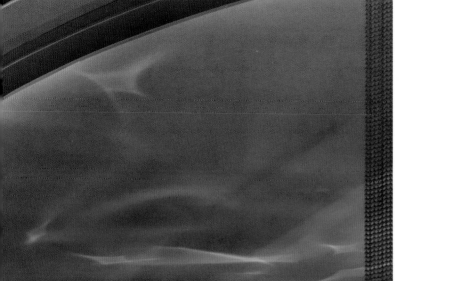

IMMERSE

W CHICAGO LAKESHORE
Chicago

The W Hotel chain has built its unrivaled reputation by staying ahead of the curve. The dazzling W Chicago Lakeshore is Will and Gray's new iteration of the brand's iconic style that daringly pushes boundaries. Meyer Davis was commissioned to renovate and redecorate the fifty-year-old, 520-room hotel (originally a banal Days Inn) with a stunning lakefront location. It provided Will and Gray the opportunity to pay homage to Chicago's legacy of architectural innovation (which includes the world's first skyscraper and America's tallest building). With skyline views on one side and the panorama of oceanic Lake Michigan on the other, the site offered a unique chance to synthesize Chicago's natural and man-made landscape—geography as destiny and inspiration.

The W Chicago Lakeshore fuses a variety of experiences in its glamorous living room–like lobby. Black and copper mirrors reconcile, animate, and expand the space. Striated Asher Grey stone floors emulate the skyline and the shadows it casts, while directing guests through the public spaces. Intimate, semiprivate conversation pods are separated by retractable, metal-beaded drapes that shimmer as the city does at night, offering flexible levels of retreat and intimacy for hanging out in the lobby. The centerpiece of the adjacent restaurant is a floating, semitransparent room-within a room—a skeletal structure of curved, mirrored strips—that creates a focal point and aspirational VIP area. The dialectic between the tranquil blue of Lake Michigan and the sturdy gray of the city's grid are literally reflected in the guest rooms, where metallic wall tiles refract the views to become abstract works of art. Sleek, sexy, and sassy, the W Chicago Lakeshore is Will and Gray's ultramodern contribution and testament to the Windy City's reputation for memorable architecture and cutting-edge style.

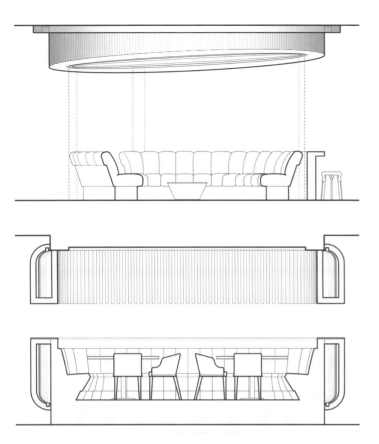

PRECEDING PAGES

Asher Grey stone floors contribute to a runway effect in the lobby. A backlit, laser-cut screen is a sparkling abstract interpretation of Chicago's urban grid.

LEFT

Drawings of one of the conversation pods in the lobby and of the semiprivate elevated dining platform that was dubbed the "oyster" by the Meyer Davis design team.

BELOW

The "oyster" is the focal point of the lounge and draws guests to the restaurant.

OPPOSITE TOP ROW

Above the bar, a polished-chrome light fixture mimics the Chicago skyline; both the bar and the banquettes are upholstered in channel-tufted leather.

OPPOSITE CENTER ROW

The wall behind the reception desk is an installation of whitewashed spray-paint cans, alluding to their invention in a Chicago suburb in 1949 and the popularity of graffiti as a form of urban expression.

OPPOSITE BOTTOM ROW

The polished-chrome pool table with a purple-felt top is the central feature of the bar area, amplifying the hotel's playful attitude; the stitching on the base of the bar relates to the illuminated screening in the lobby and restaurant.

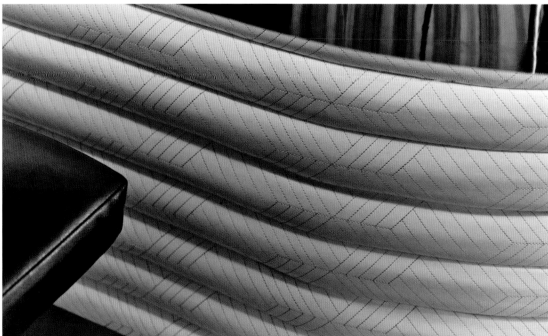

ABOVE

The watery-patterned carpet inside the semiprivate dining room is a reference to nearby Lake Michigan.

LEFT

The abstraction of the city's grid is repeated in the black-and-white carpet in the hotel's corridors. Purple lights render it black and blue.

OPPOSITE TOP LEFT

On the wall behind the bed, a photograph of the city at night by Carsten Witte was custom-printed on a reflective wall covering by Tri-Kes.

OPPOSITE TOP RIGHT

Designed as places to party, the suites are appointed with long banquettes and custom light fixtures like those you'd find in a nightclub.

OPPOSITE BOTTOM

In a suite with a custom bathtub next to the bed, the mirror-paneled headboard wall creates an intriguing view of the lakefront.

ESCAPE

THE REMEDY BAR

Vail, Colorado

When it comes to hospitality projects, Will and Gray are social engineers. Their schematics go beyond furniture groupings and fabric swatches to full-blown metaphysical forecasts for how a bar or restaurant will come to life when it's up and running. Over the years, collaborating with some of the most innovative hoteliers and restaurateurs of their generation, they have honed their instincts about human behavior and developed a proprietary formula for creating public spaces that have the warmth and friendliness of a party in a private home.

Meyer Davis's enviable track record for designing hotspots across the country attracted the management team at the Four Seasons in Vail. The goal was to transform the prosaic lobby lounge into a welcoming bar and restaurant that would be a day-into-evening hangout for registered guests and locals too. One of the designers' key moves was placing a square bar—with seating on three sides to encourage crosstalk—on axis with the hotel's front door, so the bar would function like a magnet and become the hub of the hotel.

The last thing Vail needed was another après ski lounge with a stone fireplace, plaid clubs chairs, and antler chandeliers. Meyer Davis eschewed those Rocky Mountain clichés in favor of a crisp, tailored décor with a knowing nod to jet-set resorts in the Alps. The look is a refined riff on Western style, incorporating native materials like suede, beetle kill pine, and reclaimed cedar. The enormous, two-sided, blackened-steel fireplace has a chimney clad in leather and banded in metal straps—a muscular move but a sublime one too. Saddle-leather trim on the zinc bar and leather welting on the sofa cushions are suave bespoke details. The chandeliers by Grant Larkin are a modernist take on kerosene lanterns. It was essential that the glass-and-steel fixtures be transparent so as not to obstruct the jaw-dropping views through floor-to-ceiling windows of skiers' traversing Vail Mountain—what the designers deliberately framed as the ultimate money shot.

PRECEDING PAGES

A custom two-sided blackened-steel fireplace separates the lounge and bar areas. Its chimney is wrapped in leather with metal strapping

OPPOSITE

A banquette upholstered in distressed leather is cozily set into an ebonized paneled wall.

ABOVE

The polished-zinc bar is edged in leather. The bookcase at the far end of the lounge functions as a light box.

Meyer Davis always uses a mix of seating in lounges: the leather chairs with metal frames and wood arms in the foreground are by Designlush; the Moroso chairs by the window are upholstered in an outdoor fabric that looks like linen.

ABOVE

The barstools have leather seats and velvet and leather backs The sofas are trimmed with leather welting.

OVERLEAF

Grant Larkin's blackened-metal and antique restoration-glass light fixtures do not distract from the breathtaking view of Vail Mountain.

PIONEER

1 HOTEL SOUTH BEACH

Miami Beach

Eco-conscious resorts are typically situated on pristine coastlines in countries like Costa Rica and Sri Lanka, so conceptualizing one for the heart of Miami Beach was a counterintuitive challenge. The visionary hotelier Barry Sternlicht engaged Meyer Davis to collaborate on the launch of a new luxury brand with sustainability as its guiding principle. The 1 Hotel South Beach on landmark Collins Avenue redefines the gestalt of the urban hotel experience. It's a game changer—thematically, aesthetically, programmatically.

From the instant you arrive at the reclaimed-redwood porte cochere, where thousands of tropical plants cascade down the façade, you're immersed in nature. Double-height windows at the entry create an indoor-outdoor dialectic, and walking into the lobby is like entering a gigantic terrarium. Will and Gray's design is in deliberate contrast to the hard-edged glitz of South Beach and its art deco antecedents. With crisp white upholstery, gauzy curtains, and painted banyan tree columns, the lobby is literally a breath of fresh air. As an understated urban oasis, the 1 Hotel South Beach represents a paradigm shift that Will calls "the luxury of *enough*."

The guest rooms reference the typology of surf shacks around the globe, with a sand-and-surf palette and a beach-house vibe. Overlooking the ocean or Biscayne Bay, they have hemp mattresses set against walls sheathed in driftwood-colored planks made from reclaimed pine. Upholstered daybeds or built-in sofas in white oak veneer are reminiscent of deck furniture, so you feel relaxed enough to lounge around in a wet bathing suit. One of Will and Gray's most audacious moves was knocking down the walls between the bathrooms and bedrooms, replacing them with diaphanous curtains that allow the marble showers to be private or open to the water views.

Will and Gray also designed the four oceanfront swimming pools and two Tom Colicchio restaurants (Beachcraft and the Sand Box), which echo each other, so the hotel feels like its own sustainable microclimate.

243

PRECEDING PAGES

The locally sourced coral stone numeral 1 at the reconfigured porte cochere weighs 7,500 pounds.

ABOVE

Upon entering the sunlit lobby, guests are immersed in a feeling of oceanside tranquillity. Subtle touches of nature and lush greenery blur the distinction between indoors and outdoors.

BELOW

Meyer Davis breathed new life into an existing, outdated hotel that occupies a full city block on bustling Collins Avenue. The rendering depicts how a green wall transformed the façade.

RIGHT

A detail of a mural by the local artist 2Alas, who collaborated with Plant the Future, a nature-oriented Miami boutique. Moss is growing through the mural's apertures.

BELOW

Live plants, sculptural banyan tree trunks, and New Zealand shag wool rugs enhance the hotel's focus on natural elements. LED lights on the steps guide guests through the space.

OVERLEAF LEFT

In the Tom on Collins bar, Bocci glass pendants filled with air plants hang loosely from the underside of the bar's stone overhang.

OVERLEAF RIGHT

A raised platform in the lobby, which is transformed into a stage for live bands during special events, features architectural timber screens. The slipcovered chairs are by B&B Italia.

ABOVE

The live-edge concierge desk has a teak-root base paired with torched-stump stools by Kaspar Hamacher.

OPPOSITE

The bar's lounge features a custom live-edge walnut slab table, triple-burnt stools by Andrianna Shamaris, and a wall of shelves with sculptural baskets by Brooklyn artist Doug Johnston.

ABOVE

Even though this restaurant is an interior space, the Meyer Davis design team refers to it as the "porch." It is furnished with teak- and ceramic-topped tables, and woven-jute and bleached-oak chairs.

OPPOSITE

Slatted park bench–style banquettes contribute to the indoor/outdoor aesthetic, as does the mix of teak- and ceramic-topped tables.

LEFT

The restaurant's second-floor lounge features jute rugs and saddle-leather oval chairs handmade in Texas by Garza Marfa. The custom barstools are by Asher Israelow.

RIGHT

Custom banquettes have leather and fabric cushions held in place with leather straps. The custom hanging lamps are by Axon Design.

BELOW

A collection of nature-oriented books, accessories, and artwork on a glowing bookshelf give the lounge a residential feel.

**OPPOSITE, CLOCKWISE
FROM TOP LEFT**

A progression of illuminated portals breaks
up long corridors; a woven lampshade
hangs over a live-edge white oak table
that can be used as a desk; the headboard
walls are paneled in reclaimed beetle kill
pine with custom light fixtures; a bathroom
features a white Calacatta marble shower
enclosure and a locally poured concrete
vanity; the driftwood-and-lacquered-steel
bedside lamp is by Bleu Nature.

TOP

The illuminated white oak platform
supports both the bed and built-in
sofas for lounging.

ABOVE

The subtle, natural palette blends in
with the panoramic ocean views.

TOP LEFT

The entrance to the penthouse suite has an ocean-blue distressed mirror, bleached teak-root console, and a moss wall.

TOP RIGHT

A live-edge slab headboard is juxtaposed to a beetle kill pine–paneled wall. The solid marble bedside lamp is by Hayman Bay.

ABOVE LEFT

In a corner of the penthouse suite, a chair by Hans Wegner is paired with a custom white oak bookshelf, Marset floor lamp, and shag wool rug from New Zealand.

ABOVE RIGHT

The dining room of the penthouse suite has a hand-blown Branching Bubble chandelier by Lindsey Adelman, wicker-backed chairs by Marcel Wanders, and lamps by Jørgen Gammelgaard.

ABOVE

Meyer Davis furnished the penthouse suite
with whitewashed oak paneling, a custom
sofa, and a gnarled-wood coffee table.

OVERLEAF

Shaded by a thatched roof, the live-edge
poolside bar has a white stone base.
Slipcovered sofas and antique chairs are
set into sand pits.

OPPOSITE

In a private cabana made of ipe wood, a custom natural teak daybed overlooks the ocean.

ABOVE

Meyer Davis designed the natural teak chaises that surround one of the hotel's four swimming pools. The pool deck also includes plush loungers, lanterns, and large daybeds that look as if they are floating in the pool. The planters are by Atelier Vierkant.

BELOW

A rendering of the multilevel pool decks that provide guests with a variety of public and private lounging options on the block-long exterior facing the ocean.

CHRONOLOGY

1999

MEYER DAVIS STUDIO
SoHo, New York City
First studio, at 568 Broadway

KNAUGHTY PINES ▼
Copake, New York
Gray and Chase's first home in upstate New York

2000

V BAR ▲
Las Vegas, Nevada
Sophisticated, New York-style cocktail lounge at the Venetian Hotel for nightlife impresarios David Rabin and Will Regen

2001

BEAVERKILL HOUSE ▶
Roscoe, New York
Family home in upstate New York

2004

MEYER DAVIS STUDIO
SoHo, New York City
Second studio, at 270 Lafayette Street

MAS (FARMHOUSE) ▲
SoHo, New York City
Intimate New American and French restaurant on Downing Street for Chef Galen Zamarra

2005

WORLD EXPO 2005 ▲
Nagoya, Japan
6,000-square-foot hospitality suite at the U.S. pavilion, designed in collaboration with Thom Filicia

UPTOWN APARTMENT ▲
Upper East Side, New York City
Renovation of an Upper East Side home

OSCAR DE LA RENTA
Bal Harbour, Florida
First boutique for Oscar de la Renta

OSCAR DE LA RENTA ▲
Los Angeles, California
Oscar de la Renta boutique on Melrose Place

2007

MEYER DAVIS STUDIO
SoHo, New York City
Third studio, at 155 Sixth Avenue

SKY FARM ▲
Copake, New York
Will and Kerstin's home in upstate
New York

UPSTATE HOUSE ▲
Roscoe, New York
Cozy home in upstate New York

2008

OSCAR DE LA RENTA
Athens, Greece
Design of Oscar de la Renta boutique

2009

LOCANDA VERDE ▲
Tribeca, New York City
Rustic Italian restaurant in
the Greenwich Hotel for Chef
Andrew Carmellini

UPPER EAST SIDE HOME ▲
Upper East Side, New York City
Full renovation of a townhouse for
eclectic art and furniture collectors

CAPRI HOTEL ▲
Southampton, New York
David Edelstein's seasonal boutique
hotel, including a Nobu restaurant
and a Cynthia Rowley shop

NOLITAN HOTEL
SoHo, New York City
Hotel designed in collaboration with
Grzywinski + Pons Ltd

JOHN VARVATOS BOUTIQUE
Las Vegas, Nevada

OSCAR DE LA RENTA
Dubai, UAE
Oscar de la Renta boutique in
the Dubai Mall

2010

BAIA BEACH CLUB ▲
Little Armier, Malta
Elegant destination beach club

BURGER & BARREL
SoHo, New York City
First restaurant for restaurateurs
John McDonald and Josh Picard,
on Houston Street

LAKEFRONT MODERN ▼
Copake, New York
Gray and Chase's second home
in upstate New York

2011

OSCAR DE LA RENTA
Tortuga Bay, Dominican Republic
Oscar de la Renta boutique in Tortuga
Bay Puntacana Resort & Club

THE DUTCH ◄
Miami, Florida
Miami outpost of Chef Andrew
Carmellini's restaurant in the
W South Beach Hotel

2012

MEYER TOWNHOUSE ▼
Williamsburg, Brooklyn
Will and his family's current
city residence

2013

OSCAR DE LA RENTA ▼
London, UK
Oscar de la Renta boutique on
Mount Street in Mayfair

PARAMOUNT HOTEL ▲
Time Square, New York City
Full renovation of the iconic hotel

KING & DUKE ▲
Atlanta, Georgia
First collaboration on a restaurant
with Chef/Restaurateur Ford Fry,
on Peachtree Road

HARLOW ◄
Upper East Side, New York City
Richie Notar's restaurant and event
space in the Lombardy Hotel

OSCAR DE LA RENTA ▼
Upper East Side, New York City
Renovation of the Madison
Avenue flagship

MEYER DAVIS ▲
SoHo, New York City
Fourth and current studio,
at 180 Varick Street

THE SKYLARK ▲
Garment District, New York City
Transformation of the three-story
bar and event space

TENNESSEE FARMHOUSE ▲
Nashville, Tennessee
Architecture and interior design
of a modern interpretation of a
hunting lodge

JOHN VARVATOS BOUTIQUE
Lincoln Road, Miami, Florida

2014

REGENCY BAR & GRILL ▲
Upper East Side, New York City
Renovation of the New
York City institution in
Loews Regency Hotel
on Park Avenue

ST. CECILIA ◄
Atlanta, Georgia
Ford Fry restaurant in
Buckhead

BANK & BOURBON
Philadelphia, Pennsylvania
Restaurant in the Loews
Philadelphia Hotel, featuring
a barrel-aging program

THE WAYFARER ▲
Midtown, New York City
A two-story throwback restaurant
and bar in the Quin Hotel

ISLAND HOUSE ▼
Copake, New York
Gray and Chase's third home
in upstate New York

AMAGANSETT BEACH HOUSE ◄
East Hampton, New York
Renovation of a home in
collaboration with interior designer
David Netto

W CHICAGO LAKESHORE ◄
Chicago, Illinois
Dramatic hotel renovation

BOWERY MEAT COMPANY ▼
East Village, New York City
John McDonald and Josh Capon's
steakhouse off the Bowery

MEYER DAVIS
Los Angeles, California
Meyer Davis studio in downtown LA

2015

1 HOTEL SOUTH BEACH ▲
Miami, Florida
Innovative, eco-conscious hotel renovation for Starwood Capital

LE MÉRIDIEN NEW ORLEANS ▼
New Orleans, Louisiana
French-inspired hotel renovation

SOHO LOFT
SoHo, New York City
Collaboration with Jenna Lyons on the architecture and interior design of her New York home

REMEDY BAR ▲
Vail, Colorado
Renovation of the lobby bar and lounge in the Four Seasons Vail

MEYER DAVIS
Miami, Florida
Meyer Davis studio in Miami

BEACH HOUSE ▲
East Hampton, New York
Will's design and renovation of his family beach house

UPPER EAST SIDE TOWNHOUSE ▲
Upper East Side, New York City
Architecture and interior design of a seven-level townhouse

VAUCLUSE ▼
Upper East Side, New York City
French restaurant for Chef Michael White

QUADRANT ▼
Washington, D.C.
Redesign of the lobby bar and lounge in the Ritz-Carlton Hotel

FOUR SEASONS ▲
Atlanta, Georgia
Refreshed guest rooms, event space, and a restaurant in collaboration with Ford Fry at this benchmark hotel

2016

TRIBECA LOFT ◄
Tribeca, New York City
Redesign of a sophisticated family home

MEYER DAVIS
London, UK
Meyer Davis satellite office in London

EIFFEL TOWER RESTAURANT
Macau, China
French restaurant in the Parisian Macau Hotel

FORTHCOMING

SNAPCHAT
OFFICES ◄
*Times Square,
New York City*

FOUR SEASONS
HOTEL ▲
Doha, Qatar

W HOTEL ◄
Fort Lauderdale, Florida

THE ADDRESS DOWNTOWN
DUBAI HOTEL ►
Dubai, UAE

ROSEWOOD LITTLE DIX BAY ▲
British Virgin Islands

AUBERGE BEACH RESIDENCES & SPA ▲
Fort Lauderdale, Florida

CONNOLLY HOTEL ▼
New York City

FOUR SEASONS ASTIR RESORT
Athens, Greece

CROWN SYDNEY HOTEL RESORT ▼
Sydney, Australia

WARNER PRINTING COMPANY
RESTAURANT ▲
Chicago, Illinois

THE ADDRESS DUBAI MALL HOTEL ▲
Dubai, UAE

PARK GROVE RESIDENCES ▲
Miami, Florida

PARAISO BAY RESTAURANT ◄
Miami, Florida

SOURCES

ART

Alexandria Tarver *alexandriatarver.com* | Amber Dixon *ugallery.com/amber-dixon* Anna Gaskell *akgaskell.com* | Art.com | ArtStar *artstar.com* | Bosco Sodi *boscosodi.com* | Brian Leighton *brianleighton.com* | Candida Höfer *artnet.com* Carsten Witte *carstenwitte.com* | Cecelia Phillips *ceceliaphillips.com* Cy Twombly *cytwombly.info* | Dan Colen *gagosian.com/artists/dan-colen* Doug Aitken *dougaitkenworkshop.com* | Doug Johnston *dougjohnston.net* Dustin Yellin *dustinyellin.com* | Emil Alzamora *emilalzamora.com* Enrique Battista *battista.se* | Etsy *Etsy.com* | Fred Sandback *fredsandbackarchive.org* Gabi Trinkaus *georgkargl.com/en/artist/gabi-trinkaus* | Genieve Figgis *genievefiggis.com* Getty Images Gallery *gettyimagesgallery.com* | Henry Taylor *blumandpoe.com/ artists/henry-taylor* | Irving Penn *irvingpenn.org* | Jesse Poulin *jessepoulin.com* Jimmy Marble *jimmymarble.com* | Joe Bradley *gavinbrown.biz/artists/joe_bradley/ works* | Julia Rommel *bureau-inc.com/mainsite/Artists/Julia/JuliaRommel.html* Katherine Bernhardt *canadanewyork.com/artists/katherine-bernhardt* Katherine Blackburne *katherine-blackburne.squarespace.com* | Lumas *lumas.com* Malcolm Hill *malcolmhillnyc.com* | Nate Lowman *natelowman.net* Natural Curiosities *naturalcuriosities.com* | Octavio Abúndez *galeriacurro.com/en/ artistas/ver/8/Octavio-Abndez* | Patrik Andersson *patrikandersson.com* Rachel Domm *racheldomm.com* | Sara Paloma *sarapaloma.com* | Super Rural *super-rural.com* | Tappan Collective *tappancollective.com* | Tito Trelles *titotrelles.com* Tom Borgese *tomborgese.com* | Tony Lewis *shanecampbellgallery.com/tony-lewis* Victor Fung *klughaus.net*

CARPETS & RUGS

ALT for Living *altforliving.com* | Bentley *bentleymills.com* | Delos Area Rug Solutions *delosrugs.com* | Elson & Company *elsoncompany.com* | Fibreworks *fibreworks.com* | Luke Irwin *lukeirwin.com* | Nani Chinellato *nanichinellato.com* Northwest Carpets *lexmarkhospitality.com* | Sacco Carpet *saccocarpet.com* Shaw *shawcontractgroup.com* | Signature Hospitality Carpet *signaturehospitalitycarpets.com* | Stark *starkcarpet.com* | Tailor Made Textiles *tailormadetextiles.com* | Tibetano *tibetano.com*

DESIGN STORES

1stdibs *1stdibs.com* | ABC Carpet & Home *abchome.com* | Aero *aerostudios.com* Andrianna Shamaris *andriannashamarisinc.com* | Arteriors *arteriorshome.com* Barney's *barneys.com* | Blaxsand *blaxsand.com* | Bobo Intriguing Objects *bobointriguingobjects.com* | Danish Design Store *danishdesignstore.com* | Design Within Reach *dwr.com* | Dwell Studio *dwellstudio.com* | Flair *flairhomecollection.com* From the Source *ftsny.com* | Homenature *homenature.com* | JF Chen *jfchen.com* Karkula *karkula.com* | Matter *mattermatters.com* | Monc XIII *monc13.com* Nest Interiors *nestinteriorsny.com* | Noir *noirfurniturela.com* | Plant the Future *plantthefuture.com* | Restoration Hardware *restorationhardware.com* | Suite NY *suiteny.com* | The Future Perfect *thefutureperfect.com* | TRNK *trnk-nyc.com*

FABRIC

Architex *architex-ljh.com* | Designtex *designtex.com* | Donghia *donghia.com* Dualoy Leather *dualoy.com* | Edelman Leather *edelmanleather.com* | Fabric Innovations *fabricinnovations.com* | Fabricut *fabricut.com* | Garrett Leather *garrettleather.com* | Holland & Sherry *hollandandsherry.com* | Holly Hunt *hollyhunt.com* | Jim Thompson Fabrics *jimthompsonfabrics.com* | Knoll Textiles *knoll.com* | Kravet *kravet.com* | Kvadrat *kvadrat.dk* | Larsen Fabrics *larsenfabrics.com* Lee Jofa *leejofa.com* | Loro Piana *loropiana.com* | Maharam *maharam.com* Majilite *majilite.com* | Maxwell *maxwellfabrics.com* | Mayer Fabrics *mayerfabrics.com*

Mokum *mokumtextiles.com* | Moore & Giles *mooreandgiles.com* Norbar *norbarfabrics.com* | Perennials *perennialsfabrics.com* | P/Kaufmann *pkcontract.com* | Pollack *pollackassociates.com* | Robert Allen *robertallendesign.com* Rogers & Goffigon *rogersandgoffigon.com* | Romo *romo.com* | Schumacher *fschumacher.com* | Sunbrella *sunbrella.com* | Tiger Leather *tigerleather.com* Ultrafabrics *ultrafabricsllc.com* | Valley Forge Fabrics *valleyforge.com*

FURNITURE

Arteriors *arteriorshome.com* | A. Rudin *arudin.com* | Asher Israelow *asherisraelow.com* Astoria Compass *astoriacompass.com* | Atelier Vierkant *ateliervierkant.com* B&B Italia *bebitalia.com* | BDDW *bddw.com* | Benchmark Furniture Manufacturing *bfmfg.nyc* | Bespoke Furniture *bespokefurnitureinc.com* Blue Leaf Hospitality *blueleafmiami.com* | Casamidy *casamidy.com* Caste *castedesign.com* | Century Furniture *centuryfurniture.com* | Christian Liaigre *christian-liaigre.us* | David Sutherland *davidsutherlandshowroom.com* De la Espada *delaespada.com* | Dine Rite Seating *dineriteseating.com* | Divani *livingdivani.it* | Dos Gallos *dosgallos.com* | Doug Newton *nightwoodny.com* Espasso *espasso.com* | Fresh Kills *freshkillsflagship.com* | Garza Marfa *garzamarfa.com* Genesis Hospitality Corporation *genesishospitalitycorp.com* | Gervasoni *gervasoni1882.it* | Gloster *gloster.com* | Harbour Outdoor *harbouroutdoor.com* Herman Miller *hermanmiller.com* | Holly Hunt *hollyhunt.com* | Indon International *indoninternational.com* | International Furniture Resources *ifrstudio.com* | J.A. Casillas *jacasillas.com* | Jonas Upholstery *jonasworkroom.com* Julian Chichester *julianchichester.com* | Just Plane Wood *justplanewood.com* Kartell *kartell.com* | Kaspar Hamacher *kasparhamacher.be* | Kelly Wearstler *kellywearstler.com* | Kettal *kettal.com* | Lawson-Fenning *lawsonfenning.com* Lee Industries *leeindustries.com* | Lily Jack *lilyjack.com* | LKD Woodworking *lkdwood.com* | MDC International *mdcint.com* | Meridiani *meridiani.it* | Minotti *minotti.com* | Mitchell Gold + Bob Williams *mgbwhome.com* | Moroso *moroso.it* | Munrod Upholstery *munrod.com* | NY Custom Furnishings *nycustomfurnishings.com* | Paola Lenti *paolalenti.it* | Poliform *poliformusa.com* Quality & Company *qualityandcompany.com* | Ralph Pucci International *ralphpucci.net* | ReGeneration Furniture *regenerationfurniture.com* | Richard Wrightman Design *richardwrightman.com* | Serena & Lily *serenaandlily.com* Shortell Design *shortelldesign.com* | Simon Hasan *simonhasan.com* Stellarworks *stellarworks.com* | Tom Dixon *tomdixon.net* | TUUCI *tuuci.com* Uhuru *uhurudesign.com* | Usona Home *usonahome.com* | Walters Wicker *walterswicker.com* | Wisnowski Design *wisnowskidesign.com* | Wright *wright20.com* Zen Restoration *zengeneral.com*

HARDWARE, PLUMBING, & APPLIANCES

Arakawa Hanging Systems *arakawagrip.com* | Boffi *boffi.com* | ecoFLAME *ecoflamefires.com* | E. R. Butler & Co. *erbutler.com* | Hansgrohe *hansgrohe-us.com* | ITALKRAFT *italkraft.com* | Kohler *us.kohler.com* Miele *mieleusa.com* | Rocky Mountain Hardware *rockymountainhardware.com* Waterworks *waterworks.com* | Wetstyle *wetstyle.ca*

INTERIOR FINISHES

ABC Worldwide Stone *abcworldwidestone.com* | Alternative Constructors *alternativeconstructors.com* | Ann Sacks *annsacks.com* | Artistic Tile *artistictile.com* Bendheim *bendheim.com* | Chemetal *chemetalco.com* | EcoDomo *ecodomo.com* Galaxy Glass & Stone *galaxycustom.com* | Nemo Tile *nemotile.com* | Stone Source *stonesource.com* | The Sullivan Source *sullivansource.com* | Towne & Country Flooring *tcwfloors.com* | Villa Lagoon Tile *villalagoontile.com*

LIGHTING

A. I. Design Lab *ai-designlab.com* | Artemide *artemide.com* | Axon Design *axon-design.com* | Bleu Nature *bleu-nature.fr* | BluDot *bludot.com* | Circa Lighting *circalighting.com* | Clayton Gray *claytongrayhome.com* | Contardi *contardi-italia.com* Delightfull *delightfull.eu* | Flos *usa.flos.com* | Fontana Arte *fontanaarte.com* Foscarini *foscarini.com* | Grant Larkin *grantlarkin.com* | Hallmark Lighting *hallmarklighting.com* | HB Architectural Lighting *hblightinginc.com* | iWorks *iworksus.com* | John Wigmore *johnwigmore.com* | Lindsey Adelman *lindseyadelman.com* | Manhattan Neon *manhattanneon.com* | Marset *marset.com* Modulightor *modulightor.com* | Mondo Collection *mondocollection.com* | Lukas Lighting *lukaslighting.com* | Nessen *nessenlighting.com* | O'lampia *olampia.com* Pedret Lighting *pedret.es* | Penta *pentalight.it* | Remains Lighting *remains.com* Rich Brilliant Willing *richbrilliantwilling.com* | Roll & Hill *rollandhill.com* Royal Contract Lighting *royalcontract.com* | Santa & Cole *santacole.com* Scott Daniel Design *scottdanieldesign.com* | The Noguchi Museum *shop.noguchi.org* | Van Teal *vanteal.com* | Visual Comfort & Co. *visualcomfort.com*

WALL COVERING

Flavor Paper *flavorpaper.com* | Maharam *maharam.com* Phillip Jeffries *phillipjeffries.com* | Tri-Kes *tri-kes.com* | Trove *troveline.com* Wolf Gordon *wolf-gordon.com*

CONTRACTORS

Bart Contracting Co. Inc. *bartcontracting.com* | British Boys and Associates, Inc. *britishboysmiami.com* | Carter Group *cartergroupllc.com* | Certified of N.Y., Inc. *certifiedconstruction.com* | Daniel DeMarco & Associates, Inc. *danieldemarco.com* Dean & Silva *deanandsilva.com* | Dutchman Contracting *dutchmancontracting.com* Extravega *extravega.com* | First Finish *firstfinish.net* | Hecho Inc. *hechoinc.com* Plaza Construction *plazaconstruction.com* | Portview *portview.co.uk* Shawmut *shawmut.com* | Structure NYC *structure-nyc.com* | MG & Company *mgandcompany.com* | The Moon Group *moongroupinc.com*

CONSULTANTS & SERVICES

Advanced Millwork *advancedmillwork.net* | Audio Command Systems *audiocommand.com* | Design 27 *Design27llc@ymail.com* | Designers Workroom *designersworkroom@mail.com* | EDSA *edsaplan.com* | Gardiner & Theobald *gardiner.com* | General Art Company *generalartframing.com* | iLevel *ilevel.biz* Kugler Ning *kuglerning.com* | Lido Lighting *lidolighting.com* | L'Observatoire International *lobsintl.com* | Love & War *loveandwar.com* | Maison Papercut *maisonpapercut.com* | Reveal Design Group *revealdesigngroup.com* Solid Color *solidcolorinc.com*

Gray Davis
Will Meyer
Abbie Slade
Abby Parker
Alena Field
Allison De Avila
Amanda Davis
Amanda Tomlinson
Amelia Munning
Ana Ruth Kimbrough
Andrea Smith
Andres Lamos
Angie Han
Barbara Martin
Betsy Trabue
Blain Kimbrough
Blanka Laki
Brad Krefman
Brandon Smith
Brett Bowers
Carly Keeling
Chancllc Drury
Chase Booth
Chin Lau
Chrysostomos Theodoropoulos
Danielle Walish
David Frazier
David Ries
DiAnna Dezago
Donna Dressel
Donna Lee
Elisabeth Robertson
Elizabeth Bolognino
Elizabeth Cobey
Elizabeth Curry
Elizabeth Harrison
Emily Ghadban
Eri Nagasaka
Eric Appel
Erica Alonzo
Geoff Hurst
Glenn Timmins
Grace Escaño-Maniatis
Gretchen Stump
Guillermo Salazar
Hawley Braswell
Holly Cornell
Hyeyoon Yoon
Ines Larrea Villanueva
Inigo Irureta
James Culbertson
Jamie Williams
Jason Golob
Jeff Buan
Jennifer Kimura
Jessica Viciedo
John Hunter
John Wofford
Joseph D'Airo
Joseph Roberts
Josh Mason
Josh Suckle
Juan Alonso
Julia Lucas Fria

Justyna Solarz
Katherine Kim
Kathleen Hudson
Katie McPherson
Kelly Ardoin
Kimberly Gerber
Kimberly Payne Allen
Kristen Cochran
Lauren Williams
Leah Nuzum
Leah Tran
Lindsay Crittenden
Linette Chang
Liz Cobey
Louisa Corbett
Luciana Conti
Lucy Harris
Luke Woodward
Maddison Hewitt
Madeline Winer
Madlin Cowart
Mae Aldhurais
Maggie Dawson
Maggie Waltemath
Mary Coleman Rogers
Mary Therese Yamamoto
Meaghan Apfel
Mei Fung Lau
Melita Issa
Mike Casey
Morgan Chu
Myriam Yee
Natalie Kotin
Nicole Hoppenworth
Nok Soubannarath
Oriane Saines
Patrick Martin
Pedro Barillas
Rachel Teplow
Rebecca Hernandez
Reece Tucker
Ricardo Cajigas
Rhys Gilbertson
Ryan Alward
Sam Moorkamp
Santiago Hinojos Reyes
Scott Traller
Sean Dempster
Shannon Senyk
Sharon Lim
Sharone Piontkowski
Simone Brahinsky
Sissy Bishop Austin
Sofia Idoate
Sonya Cheng
Sophia Chen
Susan Nugraha
Tehillah Braun
Terrill Keiner
Traci Dupilka
Virginia Bell
Wanda Ho
Zachary Zimmerman
Zaved Khadem

ACKNOWLEDGMENTS

The experience of publishing this book has given us the much-needed opportunity to reflect on our past, appreciate the present, and dream together about the future.

First, we have the ongoing pleasure of designing for luminaries in many fields, and we are grateful to our clients, who have heralded our work, offered us unique and exciting challenges, and allowed us to feature their public and private places on these pages. To them we say, "Our interiors reflect you, and we love all of them."

Second, we'd like to thank our agent, Jane Creech, who helped us navigate the publishing world. In addition, we feel very lucky to have met Dan Shaw, who allowed us to experience our work through fresh eyes. Dan has said things about our work that we ourselves strived to articulate. We would like to thank Mark Magowan at Vendome Press for the amazing opportunity to share this collection of work. We are eternally grateful for his guidance, along with that of his whip-smart team: Jackie Decter, Celia Fuller, Jim Spivey, and Dana Cole. We want to thank David Netto for writing a foreword from his unique perspective. David, our ideal collaborator, is an overall force in the design world whom we are humbled to consider a friend. Also, thank you to Rebecca Hernandez and Madlin Cowart, who have worked with us to gather the materials needed to make this happen and edit each draft in great detail. Each of these people has given us their support, patience, and counsel in the creation of this book.

Collaboration is crucial to what we do. Besides the wonderful relationships with our clients, we also want to mention the other designers who have been fantastic partners in some of the spaces you see here: Ray Booth and Jamie Stream, Nathan Litera, Jenna Lyons, and David Netto, in the chapters "Layer," "Imagine," "Inspire," and "Play," respectively.

A special note of gratitude to the extraordinary photographers we have had the pleasure of working with over the years and whose shots fill these pages: Melanie Acevedo, Michel Arnaud, Paul Costello, Bryan Derballa, Eric Laignel, Andrew Thomas Lee, Paul Massey, Rachel Paul, and Don Riddle, among others. You all play such an integral role in the lifespan of the work we do, and we appreciate the energy it takes to get it right every time. We also want to recognize Corvin Matei, whose incredible hand renderings help us express our projects often before they are created, as well as Sven Peters, Guido Elgueta, and the team at Maison Papecut, who help us put our best feet forward.

We are also thankful for the various publications and competitions throughout the world that have shared our projects with the global design community: *Interior Design, Architectural Digest, Livingetc, Departures, Wallpaper, Vanity Fair, Casa Vogue, Hospitality Design, Wall Street Journal, Financial Times, New York Times, Elle Decor,* and *House Beautiful,* to name a few. A special thank you also to Louisa Corbett, for championing our studio to the world and supporting us as a friend.

Of course, we thank the entire roster of talented architects, designers, and administrators who have worked for Meyer Davis over the years and with us now. You each know who you are and that we would not be where we are without your creativity, motivation, sense of humor, and plain old hard work. Our inspiration comes from you!

We would also like to thank all of our mentors, from our high school art teachers, to our professors at Auburn, to the amazing architects and designers we have both worked for and respect so much. And of course, we thank our colleagues in this industry and friends who have encouraged our work throughout the years.

Finally—and most importantly—we both dedicate this book to our families, who have supported us throughout our life and motivated us to continue to challenge ourselves. To our parents and siblings, as well as our amazing partners, Kerstin and Chase, who excuse our crazy schedules and keep us sane.

Here's hoping that we will have many more beautiful projects to share with the world in the next fifteen years!

Will and Gray

PHOTO CREDITS

Melanie Acevedo: pages 23 center row center, 32–39; **Michael Arnaud**: front cover; pages 4–7, 12–18, 20–21, 22 top row center, center row right, bottom row left, 23 center row center, 40–51, 60–65, 76–106, 107 left, 148 center row left, 149 center row right, 158–67, 186–93, 210–19. **Paul Costello**: pages 22 top row right, center row left, 23 top row right, bottom row center and right, 52–59, 107 right, 108–13, 148 bottom row left; **Nigel Cox**: page 23 top row left; **Bryan Derballa**: pages 114–23; **Eric Laignel**: pages 2–3, 8–9, 22 bottom row center, 23 center row right, 66–75, 136–47, 148 top row center and right, center row center, bottom row center, 149 top row left and right, bottom row right, 168–70, 176–85, 200–209, 220–32, 242–61; **Ryan Lavine**: page 171; **Andrew Thomas Lee**: pages 148 center row right, 149 bottom row center, 150–57, 194–99; Paul Massey: pages 172–75; **Michael Mundy**: pages 10, 24–31; **Rachel Paul**: back cover; pages 1, 23 top row center, center row left, 124–35, 272; **Greg Powers**: page 149 bottom row left; **Don Riddle**: pages 234–41; **Gabriele Stabile**: pages 148 bottom row right, 149 center row left; **William Waldron**: pages 22 top row left, 23 bottom row left; **Julian Wass**: page 22 bottom row right

RENDERINGS
Corvin Matei: pages 40, 72, 120, 156, 174, 180–81, 193, 205
Meyer Davis: pages 100, 244–45, 260–61

DRAWINGS
Meyer Davis: pages 88, 96, 97, 134, 152, 219, 222, 226

Best efforts were made to verify all photo credits. Any oversight was unintentional and should be brought to the publisher's attention so that it can be corrected in a future printing.

Library of Congress Cataloging-in-Publication Data

Names: Meyer, Will (Architect), author. | Davis, Gray (Architect), author.
Title: Made to measure : Meyer Davis, architecture and interiors / Will Meyer and Gray Davis ; with Dan Shaw ; foreword by David Netto.
Description: New York : Vendome Press, 2016.
Identifiers: LCCN 2016026525 | ISBN 9780865653283 (hardback)
Subjects: LCSH: Meyer Davis (Firm) | Architecture–United States–Themes, motives. | Interior decoration–United States–Themes, motives. | BISAC: ARCHITECTURE / Interior Design / General. | DESIGN / Interior Decorating. | ARCHITECTURE / Individual Architects & Firms / General.
Classification: LCC NA737.M48 A4 2016 | DDC 720.973–dc23
LC record available at https://lccn.loc.gov/2016026525

This book was produced using acid-free paper, processed chlorine free, and printed with soy-based inks.

Printed in China by OGI
First printing

First published in the
United States of America by
THE VENDOME PRESS
www.vendomepress.com

Copyright © 2016 Meyer Davis
Text copyright © 2016 Dan Shaw
Foreword copyright © 2016 David Netto

ISBN 978-0-86565-328-3

EDITOR: Jacqueline Decter
PRODUCTION DIRECTOR: Jim Spivey
DESIGNER: Celia Fuller

PAGE 1
The hallway leading to the master suite in a contemporary glass-and-stone farmhouse in Tennessee.

PAGES 2-3
The swimming pool complex at the 1 Hotel South Beach, Miami.

PAGES 4-5
The view from the second-floor lounge at the Wayfarer, New York City.

PAGES 6-7
The master bedroom at Island House, Copake Lake, New York.

PAGES 8-9
The six-story staircase in an Upper East Side townhouse.

PAGE 10
The office at Knaughty Pines, Copake, New York.